BEAUTIFUL ENGINES

Treasures of the Internal Combustion Century

Stan Grayson

DEVEREUX BOOKS

Marblehead, Massachusetts

Published by Devereux Books
PO Box 503
Marblehead, MA 01945

Internet address: www.devereuxbooks.com

Library of Congress Cataloging in Publication Data

Grayson, Stan, 1945 –
Beautiful Engines : treasures of the internal combustion century / Stan Grayson.
p. cm.
ISBN 1-928862-03-9
1. Internal combustion engines—History. I. Title
TJ753.G73 2001
621.43—dc21   00-060225

Title page art: This fine pair of 'Frisco Standard six-cylinder engines was used to drive standby pumps at the water works in San Jose, California.

Book design by Alyssa Morris

Printed in Singapore

Contents

The Seminal Machine — **LENOIR**..6

A Better Engine than Lenoir's — **OTTO AND LANGEN** 12

Otto Gets There First — **MASCHINENFABRIK DEUTZ** 16

Small Power, Big Success — **SOMBART (DE BISSCHOP)** 20

The Great Team — **DAIMLER AND MAYBACH**...............................24

England Enters the Internal Combustion Century — **CROSSLEY BROTHERS** 30

The Otto Comes to America — **SCHLEICHER, SCHUMM, & CO.** 32

The Wandering Pioneer — **SINTZ** 36

The Tragedy of Invention — **REGAN** 38

"Over 200 in Actual Operation" — **PACIFIC**...............................40

The Product of a Marvelous Man — **DANIEL BEST** 44

A Stroke of Genius from Baltimore — **WHITE & MIDDLETON** 46

Pioneer of the Oil Fields — **REID** 50

A Peculiar Marvel — **THE SPRINGFIELD** 54

The German Immigrants' Engine — **CHARTER** 56

The Great Idea — **DIESEL** 60

A Model of Simplicity — **OLDS** 64

Pumping Power and More — **SAMSON** 68

Big Power for a New Century — **NEW ERA**................................71

The Industrialist's Vision — **FAIRBANKS-MORSE** 74

New England Classic — **LATHROP** 78

The Titan from Chicago — **INTERNATIONAL HARVESTER** 80

"Not Like Others" — **WESTERN**...82

"To Build the Best Engine We Know How" — **UNION** 86

A Classic of Endurance and Power — **NIAGARA** 88

The Stalwart of Springfield — **FOOS** 90

Straight Shooter from America's Heartland — **WITTE** 92

Power Comes to the Farm — **GRAY** 96

From Telephones to Engines — **PALMER BROTHERS**...................98

The Engine Named for a Road — **SPEEDWAY** 100

The Fisherman's Friend — **HICKS** 104

The Pioneer Diesel from Oakland — **ATLAS-IMPERIAL** 108

Bridgeport's Finest — **WOLVERINE**...110

Acknowledgments

I must thank, first of all, the owners whose engines appear in this book. All were gracious with their time, knowledge and, in some cases, important pieces of literature. In particular, on the West Coast, Greg Johnson was unfailing in his support and enthusiasm for this complex project. In New England, John Rex shared with me his remarkable library and deep understanding of several engines. Captain Larry Mahan of the schooner *Larinda* and Captain Chris Seitz also went "the extra mile." Special thanks are due to Preston Foster who supplied both technical information and offered the support of the Coolspring Power Museum, and also to photographer and engine enthusiast Bill Hazzard. Individuals who offered specific research assistance included Danny Acierno, Lou Deering, Wayne Grenning, Terry Hathaway, Roger Kriebel, Edward L. Middleton, Margaret Reid, and Greg Prokopchuk. A special thanks, too, to my wife Constance for her editing of the manuscript.

As one who has been involved in researching and writing about the automobile and engine industries for nearly 30 years, I can only lament the decline in service and responsiveness of several large museums whose collections house marvelous, if vastly under-appreciated, treasures of the internal combustion century. However, the staffs at several other museums worked hard to overcome the barriers of distance and supply needed material. These included the German Museum in Munich, the Mercedes-Benz Museum in Stuttgart, and Museum Arts et Metiers in Paris. Several smaller museums and historical societies were especially helpful. Among them were the Baltimore Museum of Industry, the San Leandro Public Library, the Oldsmobile History Center, the Drake Well Museum in Titusville, Pennsylvania, the Charles Hosmer Morse Museum of American Art in Winter Park, Florida, Scott Peters of the Michigan Historical Museum, Virginia Weygandt of the Clark Country Historical Society, and Lee Grady of the State Historical Society of Wisconsin.

Sources: For the most part, I have relied upon magazines and brochures of the epoch for much of the research material relating to the engines, people, and companies. For the Otto and Daimler sections, I referred to the important but long out-of-print *Story of the German Internal Combustion Engine* by Friederich Sass. Also serving as reference was *Internal Fire* by C. Lyle Cummins, Jr. and several editions of *Bores & Strokes* published by the Coolspring Power Museum.

The Photographers:

Lindi Apgar: Page 109 right
Gary Beem: Pages 38, 39, 44, 45, 68-70.
Bruce Beaton: Pages 100-102.
Lance Burghardt: Pages 20, 21, 54, 55.
Robert Critz: Pages 40, 41, 82-84, 108, 109.
Richard Durgee: Pages 88, 89.
Michael Garmin: Pages 74, 76, 78, 79.
Bill Hazzard: Pages 12, 14, 16, 19, 30, 31, 32-34, 36, 46-47, 50-51, 56-58, 64, 66, 77, 80, 81, 86, 87, 90, 91, 92-94.
Ed Malitsky: Pages 71, 72, 96, 98, 110, 111.
Tina Mori: Pages 104-107.

Introduction

The twentieth century has often been called the "internal combustion century," and for good reason. With the invention and production of practical internal combustion engines, virtually every facet of life and every industry was changed. Initially tied to piped-in illuminating gas as its power source, the internal combustion engine first impacted how work was done in factories, businesses, and homes. Later, when freed of a permanent location by the ability to burn liquid fuel, internal combustion engines spread far and wide. They replaced steam engines on farms, at mines, in oil fields, and they brought the miracle of electrification to rural homes. On the water, the engines immediately changed the age-old craft of the fisherman and the economics of the fisheries. Development of automobiles and airplanes followed.

To some readers, the early dates of a few of the engines included in this book may come as a surprise. In fact, the "internal combustion century" actually began at about the same time as the American Civil War, although it would take another three decades of innovation before production was begun on a wide scale. This book focuses on the period 1861 to 1928. Not included here are the precursors to the pioneers developed by Lenoir and Otto.

While the importance of internal combustion has been widely recognized in a general sense, the details of the engines themselves and the place of each in advancing the overall technology has thus far been appreciated only on a more limited scale. Yet, the mechanical genius of the internal combustion engine is a source of wonder that is only likely to increase as time puts more distance between the observer and the bygone engineer. This book was created, in part, to make the fascinating mechanics of the engines more accessible to a wider audience.

If the engines themselves are worthy of study, so are the stories of the men and companies behind the internal combustion movement. These are tales full of genius and drama played out by the famous and the forgotten alike. But whether they lived and died in obscurity or were celebrated for their achievements, the lives of the internal combustion pioneers reveal perseverance, inspiration, and the development of incredibly original solutions to the common challenges of their calling.

Ultimately, this book was created to recognize, in one place, the achievements of those first generations of engine men and to present the internal combustion engine in all its artful glory. How, it is fair to ask, was the decision made on what engines to include, or which to leave out? The answer is that the machines assembled here are a representative collection that includes some of the most important engines ever built, as well as others that are in all respects "everyday" machines. Some engines are correctly restored while others are in their original condition. All are remarkably rare survivors of the thousands of their like that left the factory, did their work, and then were abandoned or consigned to a scrap drive.

There are numerous engines that were considered for inclusion but didn't make it. This is no reflection on their importance. Rather, it more typically reflects the accessibility of a specific engine for the demanding sort of photography presented here. Other considerations included publishing deadlines and the simple economics of a lavish book of this type.

It doubtless seems odd, to many, that important objects as diverse as Windsor chairs and automobiles have been the subjects of such a treatment as this one — not to mention their celebration in museum collections — while engines have not. In part, this may result from the more easily accessible nature of those former objects. Engines require some study, and they are not familiar to most in the same sense as are many other antiques or collectibles. Their impact, however, has been too enormous to ignore, although curators in several important museums have managed to largely do so. It is my hope that this book may help to bring the wonder of these old engines to a wider audience and prompt increased focus on the industrial archaeology that the internal combustion field so richly deserves.

Stan Grayson
Marblehead, Massachusetts
October, 2000

The Seminal Machine
LENOIR

A French-built Lenoir of 1861. Air enters the intake-side slide valve through the brass tube beside the cylinder. A lever to control the amount of gas admitted is seen on the manifold. This engine is equipped with a vertical governor that acts on the gas inlet pipe. The slide valve is clearly visible in its forward-most position. (Musee des Arts et Metiers – CNAM, Paris/Photo)

Owner: Musee Arts et Metiers – CNAM, Paris
Manufacturer: La Societe des Moteurs Lenoir
Year: 1861
Fuel: City gas
Type: Double-acting, non-compression
Ignition: Electric
Height: 66" (170 cm)
Width: 38" (97 cm)
Length: 93" (237.5 cm)
Weight: 1768 lbs. (800 kg)

Jean Joseph Etienne Lenoir (1822–1900)

On March 9, 1860, just over a year before the start of the American Civil War, a French science magazine named *Cosmos* published an article about a one-horsepower internal combustion engine that was destined to change the world. Six weeks earlier on January 24th, in Paris, the engine's inventor had applied for a patent on a machine that "consists first in the employment of illuminating gas in combination with air, ignited by electricity, as a motive force. Second, in the construction of a machine intended to employ this said gas." Here it was at last — an apparently practical engine that used something other than steam and solid fuel to produce work. It could be started or stopped conveniently, ran with little noise, and, of course, needed no fire or boiler.

This engraving shows an 1867 Lenoir rigged to a drive belt. Visible inside the spokes of the band wheel is the rotary-style distributor. Also visible are the wires leading to what were variously called the "contact points," the "sparking plugs," or, in the U.S., the "inflammators." The gas inlet lever is seen on the manifold beneath the valve chest. Air would enter once the cap on the tube atop the near-side valve chest was removed. (Photo: Deutsches Museum, München)

Even as controversies sprang up regarding the merits, or demerits, of the engine by comparison to one developed but abandoned as unsatisfactory by another Parisian, Pierre Hugon, the publicist for Lenoir's machine mounted a big marketing campaign. The publicist's name was Gautier, and he formed the company that would build and sell the engine, capitalizing the endeavor with two million gold francs. By May, Gautier had seen to the installation of a four-horsepower Lenoir in a workshop at 35 rue Rousselet, and this spot in Paris must mark the commercial beginning of the internal combustion century. People also read of the engine in a widely circulated magazine named *L'Illustration* and went to the rue Rousselet to see it.

By the end of September, 1860, a thread manufacturer had bought and taken delivery of a Lenoir and so had an ivory turner who used his engine to operate his circular saw. Gautier continued to use the press skillfully. Reports were published abroad. In Germany, a young salesman named Nicolaus Otto would soon be reading of Lenoir's invention. Shortly, seemingly every man on earth who had ever investigated the challenge of engines or electricity would hear of the Lenoir. The following summer found the 39-year-old inventor taking people for boat rides on the Seine, embarking at the Invalides bridge and cruising along the quays where one may still stroll today and imagine the scene as it might have looked.

By the time of the great Paris Exposition of 1867, it was reported that 150 Lenoir engines were in operation in Paris alone with an equal number at work in other French locations and in foreign countries. Seven or eight were reported to have been sold in England and the same number in Russia. Engines were built under license in Germany, England, and the U.S. as well as in France. A Lenoir or two had even made its way to Peru, Chile, and Cuba. "This machine was patented in 1860, and is now in very extensive use," read the *Reports of the United States Commissioners* to the Exposition. "The gas-engine of Mr. Lenoir ... uses the direct force developed by the explosion of the mixture to produce motion, precisely as the pressure of steam is employed in the ordinary steam engine." As things worked out, the Exposition (and the Otto and Langen engine displayed there) would prove to be the end of the line for the Lenoir. Gautier, having presumably gotten the money he hoped for, sold the soon to be worthless manufacturing rights to the Lenoir to another company. Still, the Lenoir's impact had been stamped forever upon the history of internal combustion.

Jean Joseph Etienne Lenoir was born in Luxembourg on January 12, 1822. In 1838, Lenoir moved to Paris where he worked as a waiter. Despite a deficient education that had provided him with barely functional literacy skills, Lenoir's real calling was invention. He did his best to educate himself and attended classes at the Conservatory of Arts and Sciences in Paris, repository for, among other things, the world's first self-propelled vehicle, the steam-powered tractor of Cugnot built in 1769. He also met and, perhaps, came to know Alphonse Beau de Rochas who would, in 1862, set forth the theory of the four-cycle engine, but not apply it, 14 years before Nicolaus Otto.

In fact, Lenoir's interests were wide-ranging. In 1847, he received a patent for applying white enamel to the face of watches and clocks. This was followed, thanks to his interest in electricity, by patents on electric brakes for railway use and a signal system as well. Using electricity as an ignition source for his engine must have seemed a natural to Lenoir. Later, he would be recognized for his inventions relating to telegraphy.

Lenoir's engine was, in most ways, derivative of the ideas set forth by scientists and engineers with greater formal schooling and resources than he possessed. In operation, the engine made inefficient use of its illuminating gas fuel and consumed many times more gas than the 500 liters per horsepower hour that Gautier claimed. It was also wasteful of heat energy and this deficiency was well-known.

A 1/2-horsepower Lenoir needed 130 gallons of cooling water while a three-horsepower engine required 800 gallons! And despite all the water, there was no provision for adequate cooling of the piston, which caused problems with lubrication and carbon buildup. In fact, only four percent of all the heat generated by the engine was actually converted into work.

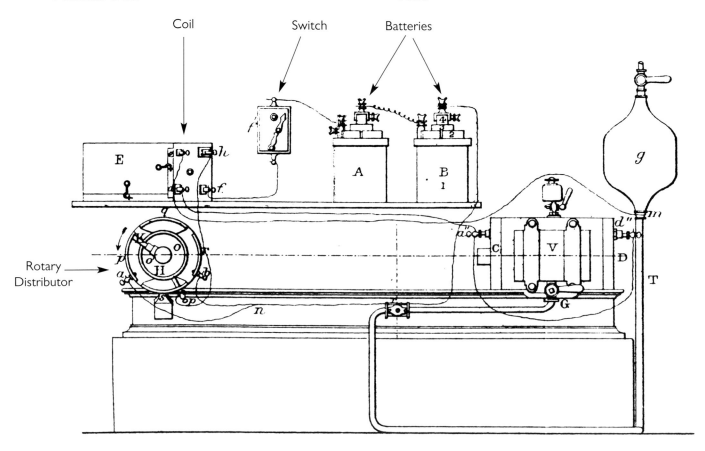

The first Lenoir built under license in Germany was this machine, made by Maschinenfabrik Koch & Co. in Leipzig in 1861. This version has the slider-type distributor, which is visible on the pedestal in the center of the engine. A flat, two-piece contact strip was in contact with the slider as it moved back and forth with the connecting rod that linked the crankshaft and piston, alternately firing the plugs. Gas enters the intake-side valve chest from the down-ward-facing manifold. The vertical exhaust manifold is seen on the opposite side (flywheel side) of the cylinder. (Photo: Deutsches Museum, München)

Another problem area involved the ignition coil. This was the coil for which Heinrich Ruhmkorff had received a prize of 50 thousand francs offered by Louis Napoleon in 1858. The coil and the batteries — very new technologies — were sources of ongoing headaches for Lenoir owners. So were wet wires and resultant misfires. If the latter occurred, the platinum points of the igniters — also known variously as spark ing plugs and "inflammators" — needed to be cleaned

and dried. Ultimately, some of the Lenoirs were scrapped; others were converted to steam operation.

Jean Lenoir's engine suffered quite a bit of criticism from more sophisticated engineers who were derisive of its lack of originality and performance. Yet it was Lenoir who overcame many personal disadvantages to conceive of an engine that drew on the work of others but resulted in a machine that with its electric ignition system was uniquely his own. We may believe that Lenoir could have been offput himself by the claims and promotion of Gautier, but Lenoir was neither a wealthy man nor did he have wealthy investors. What he needed most, one might conjecture, was a backer like Nicolaus Otto's Eugen Langen rather than Gautier. In the end, perhaps more than anything, it was the mere presence of his engine, the excitement it engendered, and the profound influence it had on the whole pioneering generation of enginemen that is Lenoir's most lasting legacy.

In June, 1864, The Lenoir Gas Engine Company was organized in New York City with a stated but probably bogus capitalization of $1 million. The company's brochure was published in 1866 and must be the oldest such document relating to the sale of internal combustion engines in America. It extolled the many potential applications for the engine, "so numerous as to suggest themselves to every practical man." These included "pumping water into hotels and at gas works; for drainage; in private houses; as an auxiliary for printing in large establishments and smaller offices; turning sewing machines; hoisting goods in warehouses; loading and unloading ships (now being done at Havre); turning shafting; lathes; lifting passengers and luggage at hotels; propelling city rail cars; for oil wells of this country, the Lenoir Gas Engine is invaluable." The brochure informed readers that the engines were being built at the Dry Dock Iron Works on East Eleventh Street and that display engines could be seen running at the company office on East Tenth Street.

How many engines were actually sold by this company is unknown but it must have been very few. James Schleicher, who helped found the company that introduced the Otto engine to America, recalled that Mr. Murray, the U.S. licensee, ascribed the Lenoir's U.S. failure to its igniter and appealed to readers of *The Scientific American* to help solve the problems. Nor were the Lenoirs inexpensive; a 1/2-horsepower model costing $500 and a four-horsepower version $1,500.

Engineers who tested and examined the Lenoir engines were careful to note that satisfactory operation depended heavily on the quality of the engine's construction. The original models built in Paris by the shop of Hipployte Marinoni were well constructed and nicely finished and worked in a satisfactory manner. If only Gautier had not engaged in his puffery,

subsequent customer expectations might not have been shattered. Writing of the Lenoir in 1894, the British engineer and two-cycle engine pioneer Dugald Clerk reported that the patent rights for England were obtained in 1860 by one J.H. Johnson. The engines were capably made by the Reading Iron Works, which, Clerk reported, actually built 100 of the machines. Clerk himself inspected a 20 year-old Lenoir that was still giving satisfactory service pumping water.

Lenoir did not grow rich from his engine. He went on to create a four-cycle engine, which he successfully defended in an Otto-related suit, and he built in 1863 an "automobile with which, in the month of September, we went to Joinville-le-Pont." This journey of seven miles from Paris and back took three hours, the machine powered by a 1 1/2 horsepower Lenoir engine that turned 100 rpm. One assumes that much of the wooden-wheeled, wooden-bodied vehicle was occupied by a water tank.

As for Lenoir himself, he became a naturalized French citizen after the Franco-Prussian War in 1871, and eventually settled into retirement in a Parisian suburb. There is no indication that his engines provided him with any particular wealth, although his other creations may have afforded him some level of income. In January, 1900, the Automobile Club of France proclaimed Lenoir as both the inventor of the internal combustion engine and of the automobile. Lenoir died later that year, on August 4th, at the age of 88.

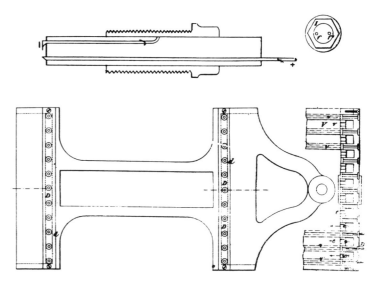

Slide valve with holes for gas/air entry

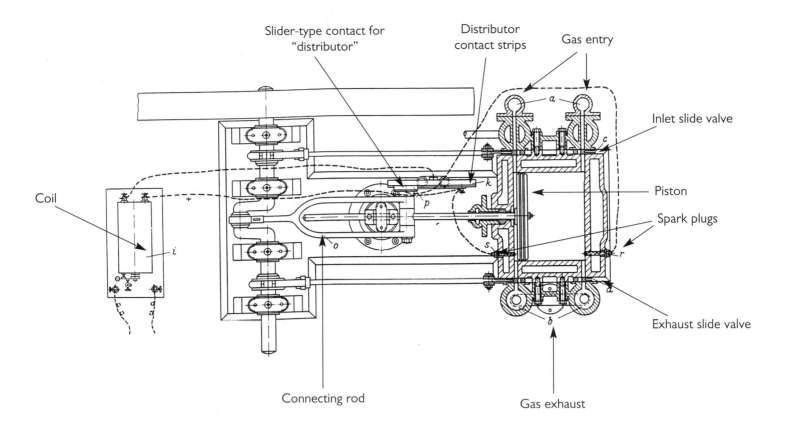

Slider-type contact for "distributor"

Distributor contact strips

Gas entry

Inlet slide valve

Coil

Piston

Spark plugs

Exhaust slide valve

Connecting rod

Gas exhaust

How the Lenoir worked:

Illuminating gas entered the valve box on the side of the cylinder. Slide valves on each side driven by eccentric rods off the crankshaft controlled the entry of gas and air (13:1 ratio) into the cylinder, and the exhaust gas out of the cylinder. As the piston moved either way towards the center of the cylinder, gas and air entered the cylinder behind it through openings uncovered by the slide valve. "The gas and air are thoroughly mixed by thus entering the cylinder in numerous separate streams," wrote the British mechanical engineer William Robinson.

When the piston reached the mid-point of the cylinder, the slide valve cut off supply of gas and air and the spark plug fired. This drove the piston towards the end of the cylinder that it was already approaching thanks to the inertia of the heavy flywheel. The process was repeated alternately on each side of the piston.

Lenoir designed different methods for interrupting the flow of electricity and causing the coil to generate a spark at the plugs. The most successful was a rotary distributor with the rotor driven by the crankshaft. Each igniter was formed of a hollow brass plug within which were two platinum wires, one insulated by porcelain.

In practice, the Lenoir was reported to be mechanically reliable, however, the spark plugs, cylinders, and pistons quickly became dirty and required regular cleaning. The batteries, too, were reportedly troublesome. Gas consumption was high.

OTTO & LANGEN

Owner: Rough & Tumble Engineers
Year of Manufacture: circa 1867
Place of Manufacture: Cologne, Germany
Type: Atmospheric
Number of Cylinders: 1
Ignition: Flame
Fuel: Town gas (now hydrogen)
Bore x Stroke: 5.85" (150 mm) x approx. 24.96" (640 mm)
HP @ RPM: 1/2 @ 80 (approx)
Weight: 1,600 lbs. (est.)
Dimensions: Approx. 9 feet high

Eugen Langen (1833–1895)

Nicolaus Otto (1832–1891)

Among the inventive geniuses profoundly impressed by the potential of Etienne Lenoir's engine was a 28 year old salesman who traveled portions of western Germany supplying grocery stores and farms with sugar, rice, and tea. Nicolaus August Otto had been a salesman for some 10 years by the summer of 1860 when his life was altered by the death of his mother in July, 1860, and by news of Lenoir's engine, which was spreading fast thanks to aggressive promotion. Otto now made a dramatic career change. No longer seeing his future as that of a salesman, he enlisted the assistance of his older brother William and devoted himself to the improvement of Lenoir's idea for a small engine that would be useful in replacing steam power and reducing the amount of manual labor required in so many industries. Thus began one of the greatest chapters in the story of internal combustion.

Otto used the city of Colgone as the base for his research and development efforts. He had a local machinist named Michael Zons construct a working model of Lenoir's engine so that he could study its operation. One result of this early study was to be Otto's ongoing and misguided concern with minimizing the shock loading imposed on an engine's piston and the long-time belief that stratifying the mixture would be necessary for safe operation.

Long before the introduction in 1876 of his four-cycle engine, Otto had acquired the capital necessary for his work by forming a partnership with the wealthy and mechanically inclined Eugen Langen whose father owned a sugar refinery in Colgone. Langen had studied engineering and physics and, like so many other mechanically minded men of the time, had been fascinated by Lenoir's engine. In February, 1864, having heard of Otto's experiments, Langen paid the inventor a visit. In March, Langen invested heavily in Otto's ideas when the two men formed N.A. Otto & Cie. In 1869, when additional capital was infused by a Hamburg businessman named Ludwig August Roosen-Runge, the company's name changed to Langen, Otto and Roosen, and the company was moved from Cologne across the Rhine river to Deutz where land was available for future expansion. Finally, in January, 1872, with the investment of significant additional capital by Langen's brothers and their sugar refinery partners, the name emerged that was to become world famous — Gasmotoren-Fabrik Deutz AG.

The engine shown here was the chief result of the initial association between Otto and Langen. In fact, it is the engine that really established the company as a commercial enterprise because it outperformed the Lenoir in all ways and demonstrated the marketability of a viable, internal combustion engine that could operate economically and reliably. The engine's merit was demonstrated in what was, at the time, perhaps the most public manner possible. At the Paris Exposition of 1867, it proved itself by far the most economical non-compression engine on display. This, then, was the first German internal combustion engine to enter serial production. It was offered in ratings of 1/4, 1/2, one, and two horsepower. The orders began arriving at Otto's shop and they immediately outstripped the production capability of the workforce of some two-dozen men and boys. Of the 22 engines ordered in 1867, only seven could be completed.

What was an atmospheric engine? The term referred to the fact that atmospheric pressure outside the engine had a role in its operation. This engine's combustion chamber (cylinder head) is actually at its

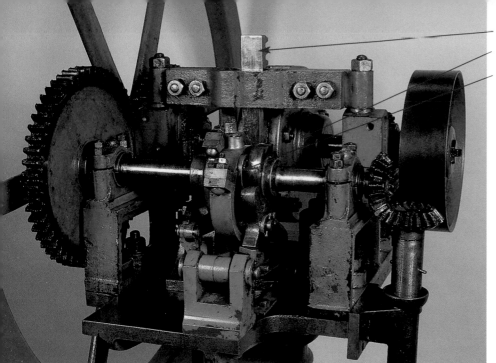

Piston rack

One-way clutch

Eccentric assembly

The eccentric assembly and clutch that engage the piston rod. The gear-driven governor is not original to the engine as built in Germany but is believed to have been added as an experiment at the Stevens Institute.

This particular engine may well have been presented by Langen in 1867 to the great engineer and designer of the Brooklyn Bridge, John A. Roebling. Langen hoped to open the U.S. market with several such seedings, but the American market was not accepting of the engine, in part because of its noise. The engine was once owned by the Stevens Institute in Hoboken, New Jersey but, after a damaging fire, the engine was presented to a private collector named William Willock who had it restored in 1978 at the Deutz dealership in New Holland, Pennsylvania. Today, it is on permanent display at the Rough & Tumble Engineers Historical Association in Kinzer, Pennsylvania. There, in the hands of a knowledgeable and sensitive membership, this important Otto and Langen is run for visitors who can only wonder at the genius it represents.

base, and the other end of the cylinder is open. Once the fuel air mixture had been exploded — in the absence of compression — a vacuum was created within the cylinder as the piston neared the top of its stroke. Atmospheric pressure, flywheel inertia, and the weight of the piston then combined to drive the piston's return stroke.

The Otto and Langen is also known as a "free piston engine." The term refers to the fact the piston is free to rise (not connected to any crankshaft) under the impulse of the exploding mixture. Yes, that long toothed rack does blast upward several feet with each piston stroke! Only when the piston descends does a one-way clutch engage the toothed rack attached to the piston, transferring energy to the output shaft that drives the flywheel.

The Otto and Langen atmospheric engine looks and is mechanically complex. For most observers, the only immediately familiar components of the machine will be the flywheel and the cylinder itself. The latter was styled in the form of a classical, Doric, fluted column, a motif that would make way in later years for a less-expensive-to-produce smooth cylinder. But, if the profusion of gear wheels, shafts, and related devices atop the cylinder are not immediately obvious in terms of their function, they are clearly beautifully made and conceived to work in harmony to produce a useful motive force.

Slide valves

Slide valves and gas piping

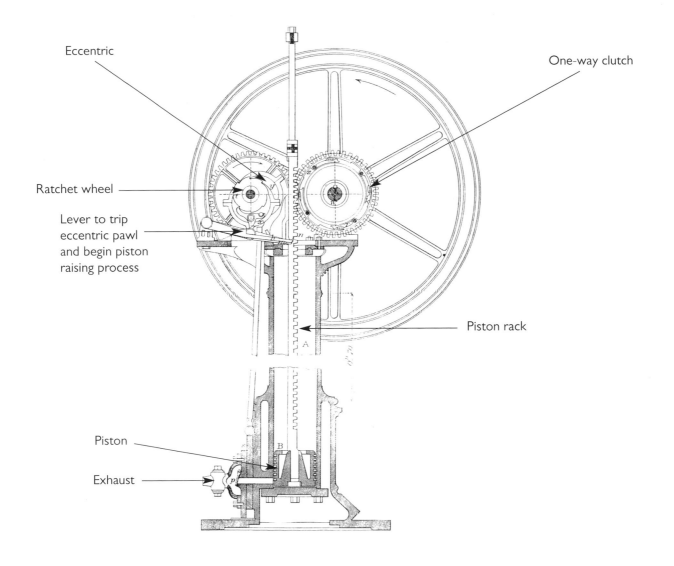

Eccentric

One-way clutch

Ratchet wheel

Lever to trip
eccentric pawl
and begin piston
raising process

Piston rack

Piston

Exhaust

How the Otto and Langen Worked

One can only wonder at the genius required to conceive and develop this engine. Although Otto did have the benefit of studying the atmospheric engine designed in Florence by Barsanti and Matteucci, the mechanical challenge of producing such an engine that would operate reliably in the hands of a commercial customer remained daunting. In fact, a trial and error process of some three years was needed to produce a viable machine. In essence, Otto and Langen had to solve the problem of how and when to move the various components needed to admit the air/fuel mixture, ignite it, and finally exhaust the burned gases. The operating process can be described as follows:

The operating cycle begins with the piston all the way down at which point the smaller slide valve uncovers the intake port and closes the exhaust passageway so that the piston's upward movement draws in the charge. (Note that other versions of the engine had only a single slide valve.)

The slide valves are timed to the movement of the piston by the two eccentrics on the gear-driven auxiliary shaft atop the cylinder column. One engages a lever that lifts the piston for the initial portion of its stroke, the intake portion. The other eccentric simultaneously operates the main slide valve allowing a precise mixture of air and fuel into the cylinder.

At the end of the intake stroke, continued movement of the main

slide valve allows the ignition flame to be in communication with the air-fuel mixture within the combustion chamber.

At the moment of ignition, the piston and rack assembly shoots upward, freely spinning the one-way clutch. A fraction of a second later, the hot gasses within the cylinder cool, resulting in a rapid reduction of pressure. Atmospheric pressure, pushing on the top of the piston through the open cylinder end, helps force the piston/rack assembly downward. The smooth-operating one-way clutch (an important innovation developed primarily by Eugen Langen) transfers the motion of the descending piston to the engine's output shaft.

The slide valve movement is halted and becomes stationary at a certain point in the engine's stroke thanks to the method by which the rack gear is moved by the cam and pawl within the eccentric mechanism. At this point, with the piston about six inches from the head, internal and external pressures have equalized and the exhaust port has been opened. Gravity now pulls the piston/rack assembly down to displace the remaining gas in the cylinder through a manual throttling valve. Engine speed is increased by opening this valve. Once the piston assembly reaches the cylinder bottom the eccentric's pawl is released, rotating the eccentrics and preparing the engine for the next cycle of operation.

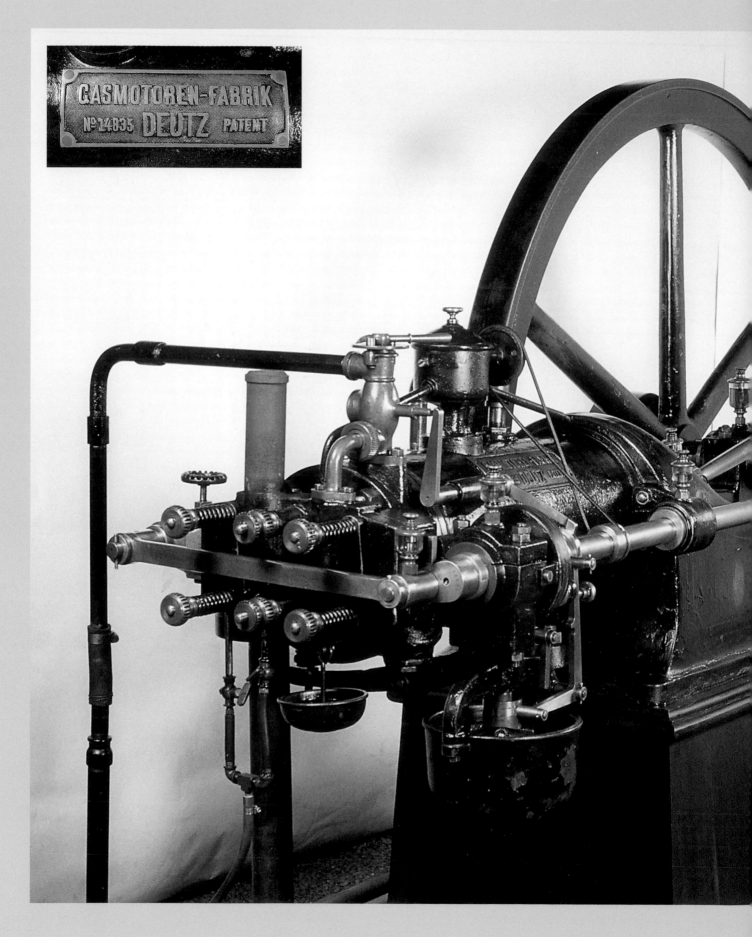

Ingenious as it was, the Otto and Langen atmospheric engine had serious limitations. Ranking high among them was the simple fact that the engine was inherently limited in terms of its power potential, three horsepower seeming to be about the most that could be expected. Otto recognized that igniting the mixture when it was under compression was key to achieving greater horsepower. In order to accomplish this within a single cylinder, Otto developed, apparently on his own, the concept for the four-cycle system of operation involving compression, ignition, expansion, and exhaust. It was a cycle accomplished by four strokes of the piston.

It was this four-cycle principle that was included in the several patents granted to Otto in 1877, although Otto's claim to the manner in which the mixture was introduced into the cylinder was also important to him. This involved his idea of "stratifying" the charge by introducing it in "layers" of varying richness. The idea was that the build up of heat and pressure in the cylinder would be gradual and protect the engine from sudden shock at ignition.

The first four-cycle engine constructed by Nicolaus Otto in 1876 was a functional but ungainly looking machine that would need a significant redesign to be commercially feasible. The task of creating a marketable version of the engine fell to Wilhelm Maybach who had by then been working at Deutz for four years. He was assisted in building the engine principally by Franz Rings, who had produced the working drawings for the prototype four-cycle Otto engine during the previous year.

Maybach's interpretation of the Otto-cycle engine was an elegant-looking machine with a nicely propor-

Owner: Greg Johnson
Manufacturer: Maschinenfabrik Deutz
Year of Manufacture: Circa 1880
Place of Manufacture: Deutz, Germany
Type: 4-cycle slide valve
Fuel: Town Gas (now propane)
Ignition: Flame
Number of Cylinders: 1
Bore x Stroke: 5.46" (140 mm) x 10.92" (280 mm)
HP @ RPM: 2 @ approximately 160
Weight: 2,200 pounds
Dimensions: 59" flywheel. Eight feet long.
Original Application: Unknown

tioned cylinder and base and a pleasing mechanical layout that followed that of the prototype. By comparison with the Otto and Langen atmospheric engine, this new four-cycle design, known as the "A" motor, operated much more quietly and efficiently. The Deutz license holder in England, Crossley Brothers, labeled the engine the "Silent Otto" to highlight the noise reduction. The "A" motor's superiority over the atmospheric engine was immediately obvious and sales of the latter engine, which had peaked during 1875-1876 now plummeted. Overnight, the Otto and Langen atmospheric engine was made obsolete.

The market for the four-cycle Otto engine was potentially immense and for the next 15 years, this engine and its derivatives would stand at the pinnacle of the German industry's production. Each year some 500 – 600 of the "A" motors were sold during the period 1876 – 1900. A total of 24,000 engines of all types were sold by Deutz in that time. That compares to some 2,649 sales for the atmospheric engine between 1867 and 1878. In general, it can be said that

the "A" underwent little change during its long production run. The entirely original treasure shown here was brought to the U.S. in 1932 for display at the Henry Ford Museum in Dearborn, Michigan. It was sold to the current owner in 1985 and is now on display at the Coolspring Power Museum in Coolspring, Pennsylvania.

The Otto patent, which was zealously protected, resulted in a temporary monopoly for Otto until it was overturned in 1886 in a lawsuit brought by Ernst and Berthold Körting. The brothers would go on to build a successful business producing large engines in Hannover. It was the Körting's lawyer who demonstrated that the four-cycle principle had been previously set forth (but not put into practice) in an unpublished patent of 1862 by the French engineer named Alphonse Beau de Rochas. With the decision against Otto, the internal combustion century could begin in even greater earnest although other bitter patent battles loomed both in Europe and the U.S.

a   camshaft
b   forward crank
c   slide valve drive shaft
c_i igniter flame chimney
d   motive gas entry
e_i exhaust valve cam lobe
f   gas valve
f_i governor
g   gas passage to slide valve
g_i governor lever
h   exhaust valve
i   exhaust pipe
m   cooling water exit
n   lubricator
o   slide valve
p   slide valve cover
q   compression springs
     (maintain sealing pressure
     on slide valve)
r   air feed pipe
u   entry passage into cylinder
     for gas and air
v   gas valve cam lobe
y   gas feed to igniter flame

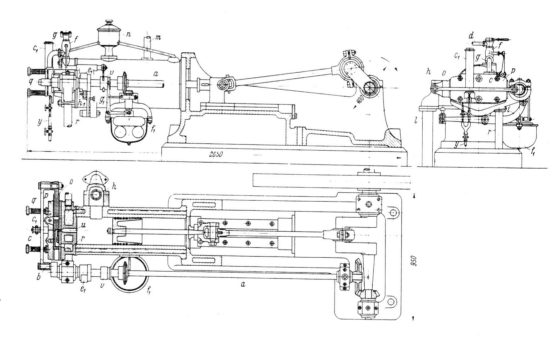

Layout of the 1876 Otto Four-cycle Engine as Refined by Wilhelm Maybach

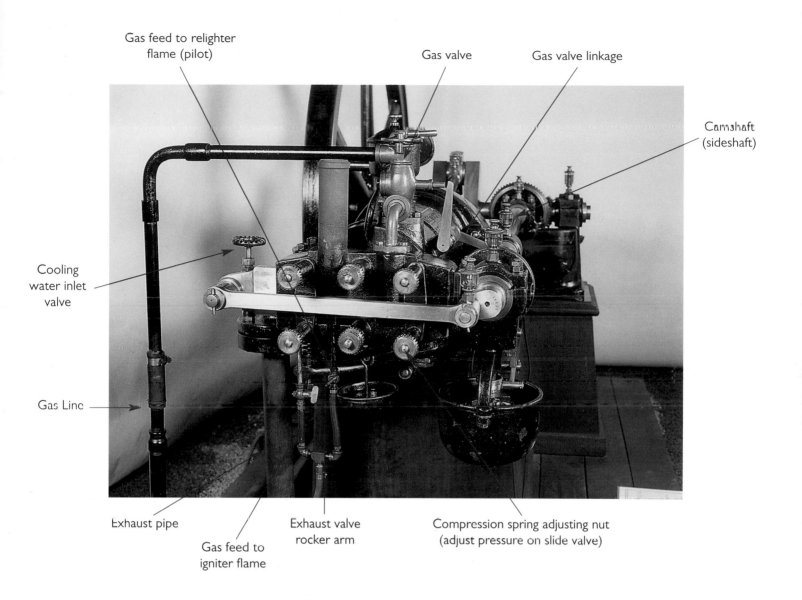

Gas feed to relighter flame (pilot)

Gas valve

Gas valve linkage

Camshaft (sideshaft)

Cooling water inlet valve

Gas Line

Exhaust pipe

Gas feed to igniter flame

Exhaust valve rocker arm

Compression spring adjusting nut (adjust pressure on slide valve)

How the Deutz "A" Motor Worked

At the heart of the engine was its sideshaft. This was gear driven at one-half the crankshaft speed by bevel gears on one end of the crank. The side shaft operated the engine's exhaust valve on one side and, via a crank on its forward end, a connecting rod that crossed the cylinder head. The connecting rod's back and forth motion worked a slide valve ingeniously designed to admit air and later expose the mixture — gas entered through a poppet valve — to the ignition flame. A hit-and-miss governor shifted the fuel valve cam away from its follower, cutting off fuel when the desired rpm was reached.

SOMBART (de Bisschop)

Owner: Tom Stockton
Year of Manufacture: 1882-1884
Place of Manufacture: Hartford, Connecticut
Type: Atmospheric
Fuel: Illuminating gas
Ignition: Flame
Number of Cylinders: 1
Bore x Stroke: 8" x 18 3/4"
HP @ RPM: 5 "manpower" (about 1/2 hp) @ 120
Dimensions: 75" high, 40" flywheel
Weight: Approximately 2,000 lbs.
Original Application: Powered a printing press
   in upstate New York

The post-Lenoir period of roughly 1865 – 1900 was an era illuminated by mechanical genius, funded by individuals and companies of varying wealth, and dominated by patents and often bitter, patent-related suits. In 1870, a Parisian inventor named Alexis de Bisschop emerged on the scene with a patented, non-compression engine that was destined to become among the most commercially successful of its type.

Although the Otto and Langen non-compression engine of 1867 had a three-year headstart on de Bisschop, the latter's focus on the market for a compact machine of the most modest power — 1/12th to one horsepower — resulted in a strong demand. In fact, power was also rated in terms of "man power" such as "four-manpower" (1/3rd hp). The engines were, in all the smaller horsepower versions, air cooled by the big fins cast into the cylinder.

The de Bisschops were manufactured in Paris by Mignon & Rouart (who had previously built Lenoir's machines) and found buyers among the many small manufacturing shops that needed a modestly powerful but reliable, economical, and comparatively inexpensive engine. This is exactly what de Bisschop's engine ($190 for the 1/3rd horsepower model) provided. Although gas consumption was high by comparison to the Otto and Langen engine, the amount of gas used

was still small and not a detriment for those who used the machine. As an example of what such an engine could do, it was reported that one ran for 47 days and nights without stopping or attention.

"A workman who has a lathe or two to keep going in his own house, or any other such small machines, commonly worked by hand or foot power, requires often enough not a tenth of a horse power to keep his work going, while the price of a suitable motor quite puts it beyond his reach," reported *The Scientific American*. "Bisschof's (sic) engines have been designed to meet these wants both as to size and price. Quite a number of them were shown at the Paris Exhibition actually at work in different parts of the building, placed there in connection with the small machines which they were driving."

Attractive features of the engine that appealed to customers included the fact that a hopper of cooling water and associated plumbing were not required. Also, the engine took up modest floor space. The offset

crankshaft was thought to increase leverage, something disputed by this machine's owner, and contribute to desirably compact overall dimensions. Of course, the engine, like the Otto and Langen and the Lenoir, ran on illuminating gas. The gas, also known as town gas, was produced by burning coal in a gas plant, and the resultant fuel was piped throughout a city for lighting purposes. It was this gas which first made possible the great rise of internal combustion.

As the fast-moving decade of the 1870s drew to its close, those wishing to enter into the manufacture of internal combustion engines found themselves scrambling either to invent a machine that would not run afoul of existing patents or sales territories or else acquire the rights to an existing engine. That is the position in which an instrument making company in Magdeburg, Gremany, found itself in 1878. When it failed to procure a license to manufacture Deutz engines, the firm of Buss and Sombart turned instead to de Bisschop (as did, in England, J.E.H. Andrew, Ltd.).

Little is known today about the firm's principals other than that Buss was the financier while Charles M. Sombart was the more technically minded partner. Apparently, however, the men also acquired rights to make and sell the engine in the United States, where the patent was registered in Buss's name. Initially, in December, 1882, the U.S. operation was established at 215 Centre Street in New York City. Production, however, seems to have taken place in Hartford, Connecticut, where the company was listed during 1884 and again from 1886 – 1888. Mr. Sombart was a highly capable engineer. He made some important improvements to the engine including a patented throttle that mixed illuminating gas and air. Also, as the de Bisschop operating principle limited the engine to its modest power outputs, Sombart developed a new two-cycle engine in 1882 and, when the Otto patent was declared void in 1886, a four-cycle. Buss and Sombart ceased to exist in 1892 when it sold its assets, principally engineering talent and a skilled workforce, to Krupp-Gerson.

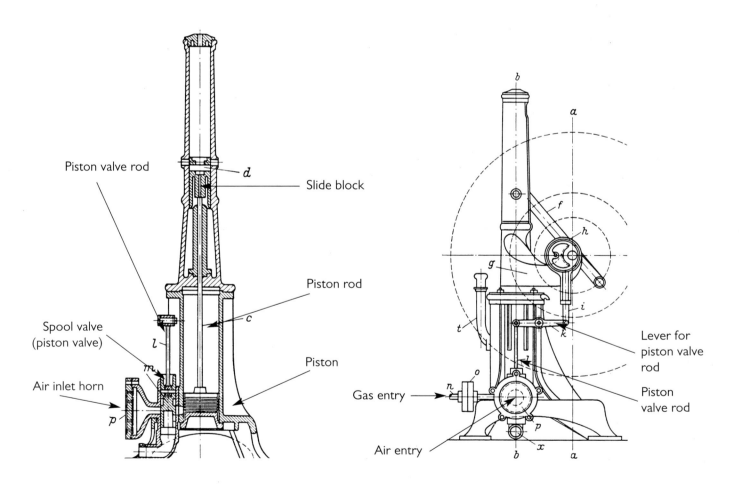

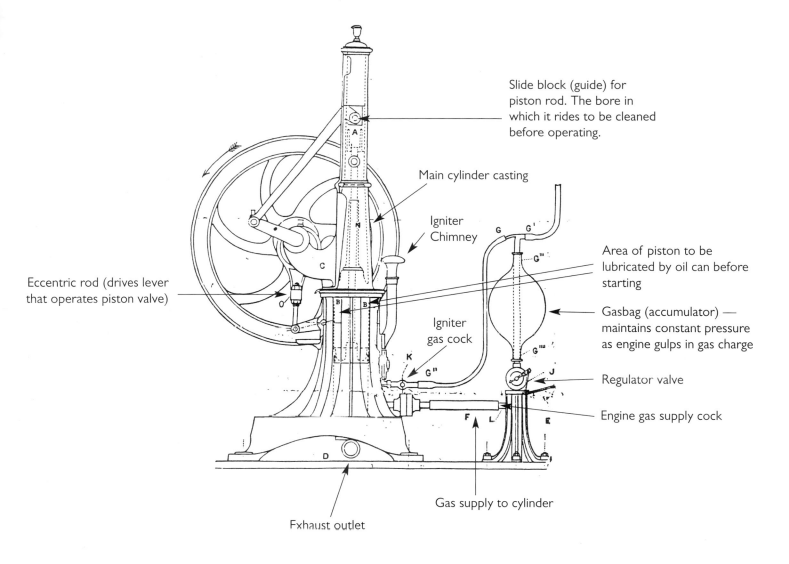

Slide block (guide) for piston rod. The bore in which it rides to be cleaned before operating.

Main cylinder casting

Igniter Chimney

Eccentric rod (drives lever that operates piston valve)

Igniter gas cock

Area of piston to be lubricated by oil can before starting

Gasbag (accumulator) — maintains constant pressure as engine gulps in gas charge

Regulator valve

Engine gas supply cock

Gas supply to cylinder

Exhaust outlet

How the Sombart Worked

A cylindrical "spool valve" (or "piston valve" because of its shape) located at the cylinder head rises and descends under the impetus of an eccentric linkage timed to the crankshaft. The valve controls the intake of mixture and the outflow of exhaust gases. On the upstroke of the piston, air and gas are drawn past rubber check valves through the spool valve into the cylinder. A third of the way up the cylinder, the piston uncovers an ignition port, exposing the mixture to the ignition flame, which is sucked in through a metal flapper valve. The resultant explosion – "rapid combustion" might be a more apt term — results in increased pressure within the cylinder. This pressure closes the flapper valve (and the check valves for air and gas entry) and drives the piston to the end of its stroke, delivering power to the crankshaft. Flywheel inertia and gravity cause the piston's downward stroke. At this point, the piston valve is rising so that it uncovers the cylinder's exhaust port, permitting exhaust gases to be expelled by the descending piston.

Why didn't the ignition flame get extinguished during the whole process? It often did, however, a "helper" or "relighter" flame located below the igniter flame and not exposed to any pressure differences, immediately rekindled the igniter jet. Speed is controlled by a quite sensitive throttle lever on the gas inlet. The engine is remarkably silent in operation if the gas mixture is correctly adjusted, the primary noise being that of the ignition port's flapper valve, that slams shut with a "clack" at ignition.

The Great Team
DAIMLER & MAYBACH

Two great pioneering duos created much of the groundwork for the internal combustion century in Germany. The first was Otto and Langen, men who focused primarily on stationary and marine engines at their Deutz Maschinenfabrik. The second was the team of Gottlieb Daimler and Wilhelm Maybach, whose ultimate achievements were made in the area of lightweight, high-speed engines for self-propelled vehicles of all sorts. One can only marvel at the depth of creative engineering and executive talent gathered in one place after Daimler and Maybach were hired at Deutz in 1872. There, Otto, Langen, Maybach and Daimler all worked together — with growing unhappiness — for almost a decade.

Gottlieb Daimler was born in Schorndorf, Germany, in 1834 and, like nearly all of those who prospered as engineers in those times, followed a career path that took him to a variety of different companies. Initially trained as a gunsmith, Daimler studied engineering from 1857-1859 in Stuttgart and then worked variously in both Germany and England. In 1867, Daimler took a new job as technical director of the machine shop at a home for boys in Reutlingen. It was a move that would result in the profound impact on both the engine and automobile industries with which his name remains associated.

One of the young men Daimler met at the church-affiliated "Brothers House" was a brilliant 21-year-old named Wilhelm Maybach. Born in 1846 in Heilbronn, Maybach lost his mother when he was just seven years old. His father died three years later, and that is how Maybach entered the boy's home. His gift for mathematics and interest in mechanics made it natural for Maybach to enter an apprenticeship at the school's machine shop, and this was supplemented by attendance at the local university where he studied physics, math, and developed an innate ability for drawing. Maybach's surviving engineering sketches and designs show a powerful ability to communicate his many original concepts with vigor and clarity.

In 1869, Gottlieb Daimler decided to accept a

Wilhelm Maybach (1846–1929)

position at the big machine works in Karlsruhe. He took Maybach with him, beginning a pattern that would be repeated several times more in the careers of both men. In 1872, when Daimler left Karlsruhe for a position with Otto and Langen as the overseer of the Deutz workshops and drafting department. He accepted the job with the understanding that Maybach would accompany him. So began an important period in the lives of all involved, a period that included the development at Deutz of the four-cycle engine. Maybach's work was far-ranging and involved projects as diverse as small, half-horsepower engines to 100-horsepower models.

Maybach's years at Deutz would prove to be exceptionally rich and prepared him to move ahead with his life's work. But it was also a period of increasing conflict and bitterness between Nicolaus Otto and Gottlieb Daimler. There were disagreements about the size of engines on which the company should concentrate and many other issues besides. Eugen Langen attempted to arbitrate the disputes, but as the months and years moved on, it was clear that Daimler would at some point have to go. Langen offered Daimler the position of director of the company's branch in Petersburg, Russia, but there was little point. On June 30, 1882, Gottlieb Daimler was dismissed from his important post at Deutz.

Here is the Daimler family together with the parents of Emma Daimler on the terrace of their home in 1885. Paul Daimler, future chief engineer of the company, sits next to his mother. (Courtesy of the Mercedes-Benz Museum)

Of course, it was to be a double loss for the Deutz factory. Wilhelm Maybach was recognized by Langen and everybody else for his great competence and value, but Maybach left with Daimler. In fact, the two had concluded a contract almost six weeks earlier for Maybach to become Daimler's chief engineer in a new venture in Canstatt. He arrived in the city in late September, 1882. There, in the now famous green house behind Daimler's villa, they commenced work on what would become the world's first high-speed, lightweight, internal combustion engine. The existing Daimler archives do not reveal when Daimler conceived the idea for such an engine, nor did the heavy engines that Deutz had been building so successfully provide much basis for the new machine. Maybach immediately was confronted by the problem of what sort of fuel to use and how to ignite it. The fuel selected was gasoline. Regarding ignition, problems with quickly drained dry cell batteries and electric ignition components led Maybach to select a hot tube as the ignition source. During the next two years, as the concepts for the engine developed, Maybach studied over 1,000 patents to be sure that the design for his ignition system had not already been claimed. In 1883, Daimler filed for a patent on the system Maybach had created for a hot tube ignition system, the tube's outer end heated by an open flame.

The first engine emerged in the middle of August, 1883. Because the garden house didn't offer the necessary equipment to actually construct the engine, it was built

The start of it all – the garden house in which Daimler and Maybach worked during the early days of developing the high-speed, internal combustion engine. (Courtesy of the Mercedes-Benz Museum)

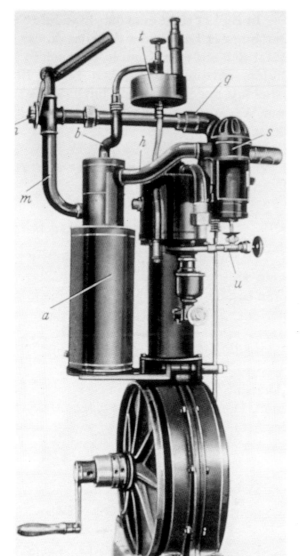

a. "Swimming" (float) carburetor
b. Feed pipe
g. Pipe to inlet valve
h. Carburetor preheater
m. Feed pipe from carburetor to air/fuel valve
s. Burner housing
t. Burner fuel reservoir
u. Burner supply pipe

Daimler 1885 "Standuhr" engine

developed it's been said with much secrecy, that formed the basis of what would become Daimler's great success. Among other things, Daimler sold the French rights to Panhard and Levassor, which soon became a major force in the automotive world.

On July 5, 1887, Gottlieb Daimler was able to move Maybach and his staff out of the garden house to a newly purchased factory. Developments of many sorts proceeded including an engine-driven street car, a new one-cylinder and V-twin engine, and a milestone for the company, Maybach's first four-cylinder engine. It may or may not have been the first four-cylinder engine ever made, but it was quite advanced in many respects, its overhead valves in particular. Intended as a marine engine, this Maybach-designed four-cylinder would be viewed decades in the future as possessing the architecture of the first modern, four-cylinder, four-cycle engine. The success achieved by Maybach and Daimler generated a need for additional capital. In November, 1890, the Daimler-Motoren-Gesellschaft (Daimler Motor Company) was formed and the new partners immediately made themselves felt in all the most undesirable ways. Apparently lacking the ability to understand either the nature of the industry or the treasure they had in Wilhelm Maybach, the new management attempted to force Maybach to accept a position and compensation wholly inappropriate. Although he negotiated the matter while a horrified Daimler watched, Maybach finally gave up. Saying that "the squeezing of the lemon has gone on long enough," Maybach quit the company in February, 1891.

It didn't take long for the new management to perceive they had alienated an irreplaceable part of the company in which they had invested, but Maybach immediately set up on his own. Soon, he and a staff were working out of rooms in Canstatt's splendid Hotel Hermann. During this period, Maybach

by the works of Heinrich Kurtz in Stuttgart and delivered to Daimler and Maybach in Canstatt. The engine was horizontal in layout and developed 1/4 horsepower at the then very high speed of 600 rpm versus the 120 – 180 of the Deutz engines. Thus began the journey that would lead the following year towards the first of the so-called Standuhr engines, which translates literally as "upright clock" but really means "pendulum clock" or "grandfather clock." In fact, the engine with its circular base and vertical cylinder did rather resemble a pendulum. It was different, always evolving versions of the Standuhr that Maybach and Daimler used to power first the famous "motorcycle" and, as the engine's sophistication increased, a motorboat and horseless carriage in 1886. It was the Standuhr engine,

Owner: Mercedes-Benz Museum

Year of Manufacture: 1885

Place of Manufacture: Germany

Type: Four-cycle

Number of Cylinders: 1

Ignition: Flame/Hot tube

Fuel: Gasoline

Bore x Stroke: 70 mm x 120 mm

HP @ RPM: 1.1 @ 650

The precursor of Maybach's spray carburetor, the Swimming Carburetor of this engine had a float to maintain fuel level. The carburetor functioned by the drawing off of vapors from the fuel it contained. The carburetor was larger than the engine's cylinder.

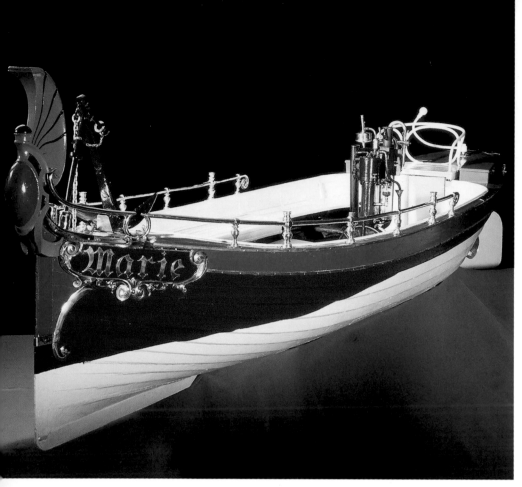

For reasons of practicality and secrecy, the most serious application of Daimler and Maybach's first engine was to a boat and a good portion of initial sales were of marine engines. In 1889, Germany's chancellor Prince Otto von Bismarck was presented with this ornate 18 foot by 4'9" launch, which was named Marie. The boat's red-painted single-cylinder version of the Daimler Standuhr produced 1 1/2 hp at 700 rpm, enough to propel Marie at about six miles per hour. The boat was returned to Daimler-Benz in 1922 by Bismarck's heirs and is now displayed at the Mercedes-Benz Museum in Stuttgart. (Courtesy of Mercedes-Benz Museum)

improved the Standuhr's effective but ungainly float carburetor with the forerunner of the modern carburetor. It was a spray-type instrument that directed fuel into the middle of the incoming air stream. The carburetor was part of the V-twin "Phoenix" engine, the most modern version yet of the Standuhr. (Maybach couldn't call the engine a Daimler for obvious reasons and perhaps chose the name to signify the legendary bird that rose from its own ashes.)

Gottlieb Daimler, meanwhile, grew increasingly frustrated with what he saw happening at the Daimler Motor Company and he distanced himself from its operation so that he could again confer with Maybach. By 1895, the lack of success at Daimler so contrasted with Maybach's brilliant success that both Gottlieb Daimler and Maybach were asked to return to the company. Finally, Maybach was named chief engineer. Back again at Daimler, Maybach found a company whose products had strayed far from the original intent and the period following his immediate return was

difficult. It resulted, however, in ever more modern and higher performance engines, and the creation of the modern format automobile with a front engine, wheel steering, and tube-type radiator. The Maybach-designed Daimler was named Mercedes, the name of the daughter of Emil Jellinek. He was the wealthy sales representative in Nice who so successfully promoted Maybach's work and Daimler's products.

After Gottlieb Daimler's death in 1900, Maybach continued on at his usual brilliant pace, which included the design of a hugely successful 90-horsepower Mercedes racing car. In the absence of his old friend Daimler, however, Maybach began running into difficulties with the board chairman who assumed control in 1903, Wilhelm Lorenz. Suddenly, Maybach found himself being cut out of planning and decision making while younger rivals assumed much of his role. Development in 1905 of a 120-horsepower race car became a flashpoint in which Emil Jellinek attempted to intervene on Maybach's part. Things continued downhill with Jellinek citing a conspiracy against the great engineer whose value far outweighed any perceived single-mindedness on Maybach's behalf. The matter ended on March 31, 1907, when Maybach resigned his position. Maybach's place as chief engineer taken by Daimler's son Paul. A year later, Jellinek left the company's board.

Wilhelm Maybach's resignation was to be, for him, another new beginning. He formed the Maybach Motor Company, initially concentrating on lightweight airship engines with his long-time friend, Count Ferdinand Zeppelin. Aircraft engines followed and later, Maybach developed the high-grade automobiles that bore his name. Wilhelm Maybach, who died in 1929, was assisted in his post-Daimler years by his son Karl, also a highly successful engineer.

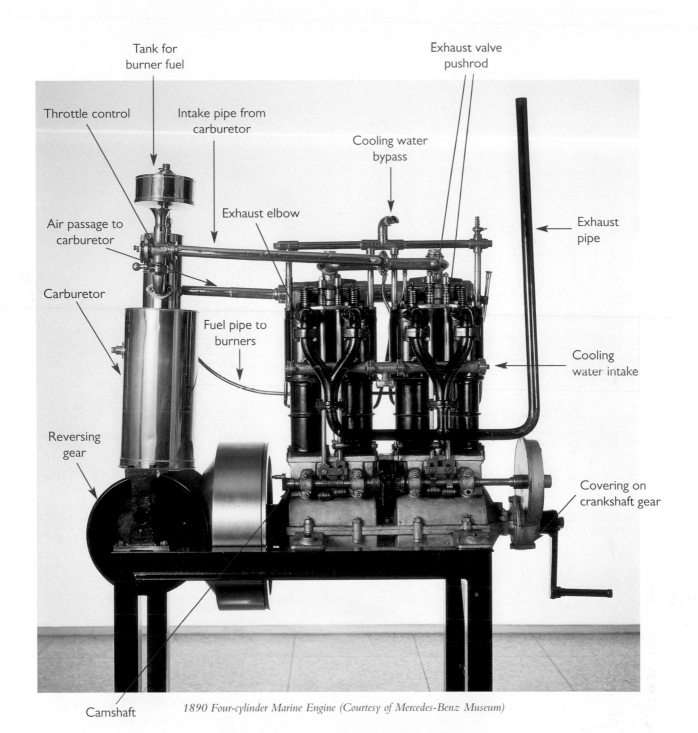

Tank for burner fuel

Throttle control

Intake pipe from carburetor

Exhaust valve pushrod

Cooling water bypass

Exhaust pipe

Air passage to carburetor

Exhaust elbow

Carburetor

Fuel pipe to burners

Cooling water intake

Reversing gear

Covering on crankshaft gear

Camshaft

1890 Four-cylinder Marine Engine (Courtesy of Mercedes-Benz Museum)

Owner: Mercedes-Benz Museum
Year of Manufacture: 1890
Place of Manufacture: Germany
Type: Four-cycle
Number of Cylinders: 4
Ignition: Hot tube
Fuel: Gasoline
Bore x Stroke: 3.12" (80 mm) x 4.68" (120 mm)
HP @ RPM: 5 @ 620
Weight: 337 lbs.

CROSSLEY BROTHERS

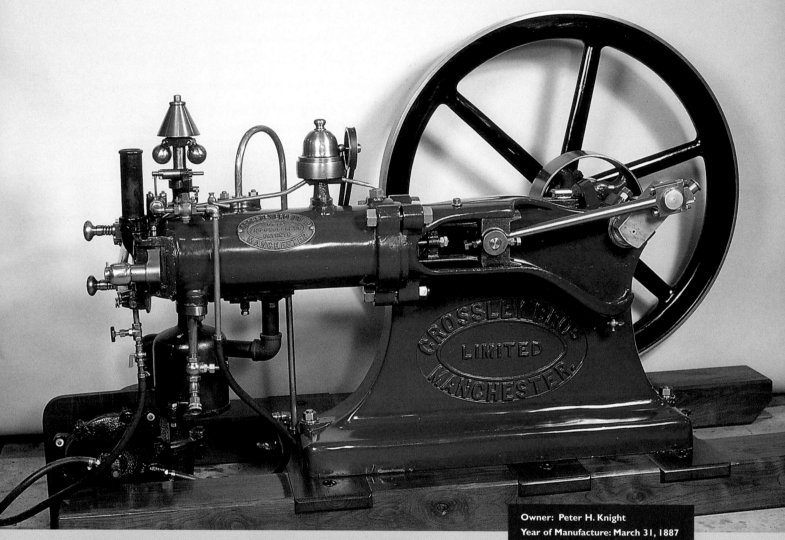

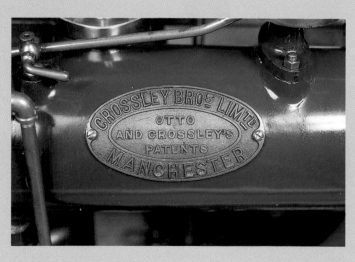

Owner: Peter H. Knight
Year of Manufacture: March 31, 1887
Place of Manufacture: Manchester, England
Type: 4-cycle slide valve (poppet exhaust) with flame ignition
Number of Cylinders: 1
Bore x Stroke: 4 3/8" x 9"
HP @ RPM: 1/2 @ 250
Fuel: Town gas (now hydrogen)
Dimensions: 42" flywheel
Original Application: Unknown, small millwright shop, etc.

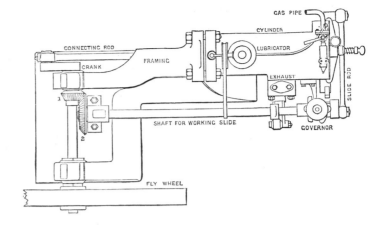

The Paris Universal Exposition of 1867, as it was officially known, was recognized as such an important event that the U.S. secretary of state authorized a commission to be sent there and to write a report of its findings. This turned out to be a very big job. The Exposition proved so overwhelming in scope that the *Commissioner's Report* was not ready for publication until 1869. "So vast was the variety of interesting objects, and so wonderful the diversity of industrial operations, which a common impulse had swept together into that single spot from every quarter of the civilized world, that the visitor, in endeavoring to make his way through the maze, found himself continually bewildered; and no one could leave it, after having devoted days and even weeks to its study, without feeling how imperfect had been his survey, and how inadequate a knowledge he had been able to gather of the great whole."

One of the fascinated visitors to this seminal event was a honeymooning Englishman named William Crossley. A year earlier, in Manchester, Crossley had joined his brother Francis in the creation of a company to produce machinery used to make rubberized clothing. In Paris, at the great Exposition, William Crossley discovered the fascinating Otto and Langen atmospheric engine. He was so impressed that he promptly had his brother Francis hurry to Paris to see the engine for himself. The result was that Crossley Brothers entered an agreement with Otto and Langen that granted them patent rights in England, the formal beginning of the internal combustion century in that country.

Both the Crossleys were adept machinists and brought a critical and inventive faculty to their new endeavor. The Crossley-built Ottos were recognized for very high quality, and the brothers made their own improvements, for which they received their own patents. Their relations with Otto were excellent and Crossley Brothers was quick to take the rights to the four-cycle Otto when it was introduced. They built their first "Crossley Silent" in March, 1877. A decade later, Crossley sent its first engine to the U.S., a big 100-horsepower machine that was followed a year later by six more and then a steady stream.

The engine shown here is a very fine example built exactly a decade later in March, 1887. Although it worked on the four-cycle principle and resembled an Otto, this Crossley model possesses a number of unique features developed by the brothers. Most important is its side-crank layout clearly visible in the photograph. The connecting rod was not located between the crankpins. Instead, it was located on one side of the crankshaft and connected to the piston with a crosshead. On the flywheel side of the engine, bevel gears drove the shaft that operated the slide valve and also drove the belt-driven oiler and, via a rocker arm, the exhaust valve.

In 1888, the Crossleys replaced these devices with poppet valves, and hot-tube ignition, while Otto's next generation engine employed electric ignition. Painted in authentic Crossley green, this well-preserved survivor has a belt-driven oiler that directs lubricant to the slide valve and the cylinder wall. This engine represents the final version of the classic, slide-valve, flame-ignition, Crossley-modified version of the Silent Otto.

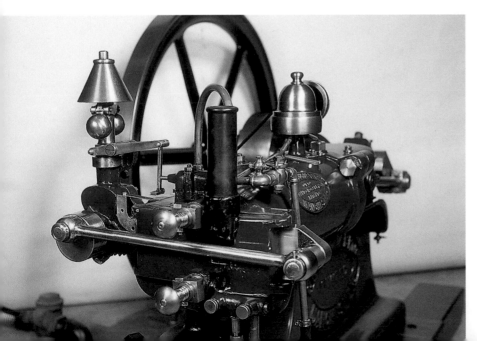

SCHLEICHER, SCHUMM & CO.

Owner: Nathan Lillibridge
Year of Manufacture: Circa 1888
Place of Manufacture: Philadelphia, Pennsylvania
Type: 4-cycle slide valve with flame ignition
Number of Cylinders: 1
Bore x Stroke: 5 5/16" x 12 1/2"
HP @ RPM: 4 @ 157
Weight: approx 3,000 lbs.
Dimensions: 51" flywheel
Original Application: Machine shop

T he market potential represented by the Deutz "A" motor was obvious to engine men everywhere. While Deutz retained all rights for manufacture and sale in the western portion of Germany, the company entered into licensing arrangements with machine works in other parts of Germany and, of course, outside the country. Licensing agreements were quickly made with firms in Austria, Holland, France, Denmark and, of course, with the Crossleys in England. Two firms in America acquired a license from Deutz. One was the machine shop of Sinker, Davis & Company in Indianapolis. Although their total production was limited, they did produce the first Otto engine built in the country and it worked for a number of years at the armory in Indianapolis.

The other and more important U.S. licensee was located in Philadelphia where Eugen Langen's brother-in-law, Jakob Schleicher, had been named representative for Deutz. In 1877, Hermann Schumm was assigned to go to Philadelphia and assist Schleicher and his sons in setting things up. A highly competent newcomer to Deutz, Schumm had worked with Maybach and Rings on the project to build the "A" motor and get it into production.

A variety of changes was made to these American-built Ottos, the more obvious being a curved base, different drive gears for the side shaft, and American threads on fasteners. In 1894, the company became known as the Otto Gas Engine Works when the Schleichers sold their interest. They had become wealthy although they learned, according to James Schleicher, that "the American market was a law to itself and a foothold could only be gained by slow degrees." The engine pictured here is one of those Ottos built by Schleicher, Schumm sometime, it is believed, around 1888.

The story of this engine is instructive, in many ways, of engine preservation in this country over the last several decades. Schleicher, Schumm serial number 2907 was purchased by a wealthy Boston-area man named Francis Blake who had invented the microphone used in Alexander Bell's telephones and thus made a fortune. Blake's four-horsepower Schleicher, Schumm cost $680 in a period when a steam engine of the same output sold for $40.

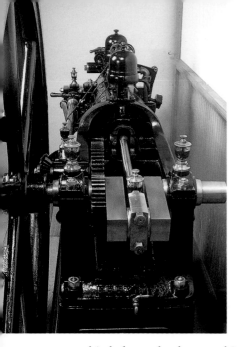

Blake purchased the engine for installation in the lavishly equipped machine shop that was among his greatest delights. Although the engine's massive 300-pound flywheel was designed to give the steady performance needed in driving a generator for lighting purposes, Blake retained gas lights in his shop and used the engine instead to drive his lathe and other machinery. The engine was still in the shop at the time of Mr. Blake's death. At some point thereafter, the family offered the shop and its contents to the Smithsonian Institution whose representatives, after inspecting this marvelous assemblage of American machinery, turned the offer down.

Instead, the Blake machine shop was purchased by a New York engine collector with the intent of installing its contents in a newly built shop on his own property. This project was never completed and, after the collector's death, the Schleicher, Schumm and the other artifacts were left exposed to the elements with predictable results. Finally, in 1991, the engine — now in need of a complete restoration — was rescued by collector Nate Lillibridge and a devoted group of engine enthusiasts. One of these men, John Rex, a scientist living in eastern Massachusetts, accepted the responsibility for bringing the Schleicher, Schumm back to life.

Today, John Rex still has the bulging notebook in which he recorded all the calculations, correspondence, and photographs that collectively tell the story of how he restored Francis Blake's old engine almost a century after it had been built in Philadelphia. He embarked on a kind of technological detective work that would take him back in time to piece together what changes Blake had made on the engine and to Canada where a larger (six horsepower), yet similar,

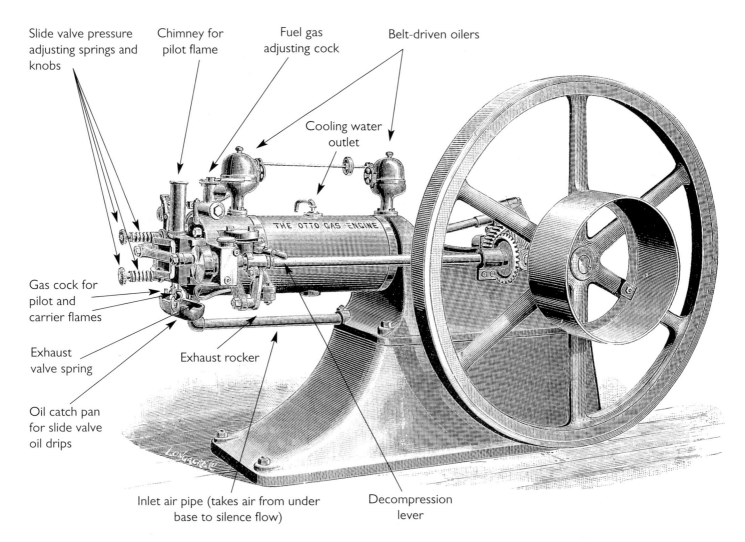

Slide valve pressure adjusting springs and knobs

Chimney for pilot flame

Fuel gas adjusting cock

Belt-driven oilers

Cooling water outlet

Gas cock for pilot and carrier flames

Exhaust valve spring

Exhaust rocker

Oil catch pan for slide valve oil drips

Inlet air pipe (takes air from under base to silence flow)

Decompression lever

THE OTTO GAS ENGINE

Schleicher, Schumm was on display and in operating order in the Ontario Science Center.

"For one thing," said Rex, "we found the engine was missing one of the gears that drives the side shaft. At some point, Mr. Blake had apparently stopped using the engine as a power source. He removed one of the bevel gears and simply drove its flywheel with an electric motor. So a new gear was needed."

The Ontario Science Center permitted Rex to visit, disassemble the Schleicher, Schumm-built Otto on display, and take all the measurements and photographs that he needed to make a new gear. Once he knew the number of teeth needed and their pitch, he made a pattern, cast a gear blank, and had a specialty shop cut the teeth.

The engine also needed new rod brasses so Rex made a pattern for those, too, from which he made new castings. The crankshaft was cleaned and the webs skinned (shaved slightly) to produce an as-new surface. The pitted flywheel was likewise machined to produce a smooth surface. Finally, the engine was repainted in its original black color and prepared to run again for the first time in decades.

"It ran terribly," said Rex. "We found that Mr. Blake had filed the exhaust cam a lot, then built it back up with solder as he tried to change the engine's cam timing. Also, the side shaft was incredibly noisy, and the museum in Canada had told us their engine was also very noisy."

Rex examined the two gears that drove the side shaft, which, in turn, operated the slide valves at the cylinder head. It soon became clear that the engine, as built by Schleicher, Schumm, was deficient in terms of the mesh of the two sideshaft drive gears. "We found the drive gear needed to be moved .032 inches for-

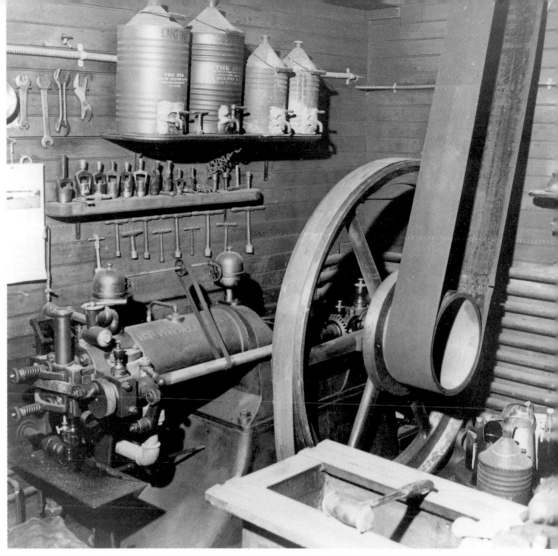

Here is the Otto as it originally looked in the machine shop of Francis Blake. (Courtesy of John Rex)

ward and .051 inches up," said Rex. He promptly made a new slightly eccentric gear shaft to provide the needed offset and perfect gear mesh.

The camshaft was another story entirely. With no four-horsepower Schleicher, Schumm camshaft available for study, Rex turned to his impressive library of engine-related books from the 19th and early 20th century. In one of them, he found drawings and tables that discussed what the cam timing would have been for an engine of the Schelicher, Schumm's era and type. Using the book as his guide, Rex designed a new camshaft lobe. When the engine was finally run again, it worked perfectly and quietly, now a Silent Otto in fact as well as name.

The Wandering Pioneer

SINTZ

Owner: Stiles Bradley

Manufacturer: Clark Sintz

Year of Manufacture: Circa 1891

Place of Manufacture: Springfield, Ohio

Type: 4-cycle

Fuel: Natural gas, illuminating gas or gasoline

Ignition: Make-and-break igniter

Number of Cylinders: 1

HP @ RPM: 5 @ 320

Dimensions: Floor space 2' 6" x 2' 6"

Original Application: Power for a loom

Of America's earliest internal combustion pioneers, few had as an impressive, convoluted, and varied career as did Clark Sintz. It was, however, a career of invention more noteworthy for its breadth and creativity rather than for any commercial success. "He was," said one of his sons in a retrospective about his gifted father, "more interested in new inventions than in developing and cashing in those that he had commercialized. His invention of the make-and-break electrical igniter would have brought him a comfortable fortune, but when the patent was ready for issue, he was experimenting with platinum hot tube ignition, and thought it a waste of money to spend the $20 for the final fee."

Clark Sintz was born in Springfield, Ohio, in 1850 and was a child prodigy. He built a tiny steam engine at age 12 and a full-size, slide-valve steam engine when he was 18. These together with a boiler were manufactured until a financial panic in the 1870s forced him to abandon the effort. Clark, who married in 1874, then proceeded to build and sell a variety of farm and steam-related equipment. The "Panic" did not prevent Sintz from attending the Philadelphia Exposition in 1876 where he was profoundly impressed by the Otto engine on display.

According to a brief and unfortunately terse article by Clark Sintz published in *Power Boating* in 1914, he built a horizontal marine engine in 1884. (Because Sintz was inconsistent about dates, it is worth noting that a son placed this event in 1887.) This engine successfully powered a 25-foot launch and marked the beginning of Sintz's development of ever-more sophisticated and practical marine engines. According to Sintz, "My next and successful engine was made early in the year 1885. I then went in the manufacture of marine gasoline engines in Springfield, Ohio. In 1891, I sold a marine gasoline engine to a party in Grand Rapids, Michigan, who after using it offered me inducements to move to Grand Rapids, and as I had no navigable water at Springfield, I concluded to move, which I did in the winter of 1892-93 and organized the Sintz Gas Engine Company."

As always with Clark Sintz, there is much left unsaid by this recounting of events. It leaves out, for example, his important association in Springfield with John Foos. Sintz was building his engines in the same building as the St. John Sewing Machine Company, which was one of Foos's several ventures. According to the

article by one of Sintz's sons: "In 1888 Sintz with John Foos and P.P. Mast of Buckeye Turbine windmill fame formed the Gas Engine Co. of Springfield, Ohio." The Gas Engine Company may have been started in 1887 and Sintz's association with Foos lasted until 1890, according to the only family record of the event, when he sold his interest.

Clark Sintz (1850 – 1922). (Courtesy of Robert Sintz)

The reason for the breakup may never be known. Sintz may well have become involved in a patent dispute with an associate or he may simply have exercised the independent streak that always drove him. He began building engines on his own during 1890 or 1891, many of which were sold by the firm of Barnhart Bros. & Spindler to print shops. A Sintz brochure of 1892 includes testimonials from several of these printers written in August and September of 1891. The engine pictured in the Sintz Gas and Gasoline Engines brochure is the model pictured here.

Clark Sintz's association with his investor in Grand Rapids was even shorter than the one with John Foos. He sold out his interest in the Sintz Gas Engine Company in 1893 to Ora J. Mulford of the Michigan Yacht and Power Company. Then, Sintz started a new business in Grand Rapids with his son Claude. This venture was called Wolverine and, although Clark Sintz sold out his interest in 1902, Wolverine would continue for decades.

Sintz continued to design engines but then he moved to Panama where he worked for two years for the United Fruit Company with which he was familiar thanks to his contacts with Charles Snyder, the man who bought Wolverine. Throughout his life, Sintz invented. He developed what was, perhaps, the first three-port, two-cycle engine, with make-and-break ignition. He built a thoroughly contemporary front-engine, wheel-steered automobile in 1902. Later, he designed an hydraulic transmission and a carburetor for the Ford Model T. Sintz retired in Waveland, Mississippi in 1916, and was struck and killed by an automobile in Bay St. Louis in 1922. He was remembered as a "tireless inventor endowed with vivid imagination. [He] was an expert mechanic, had a great sense of humor and was a great lover of outdoor life."

REGAN

Owner: Bill Santos

Year of Manufacture: Circa 1891-1892

Place of Manufacture: San Francisco, California

Type: 4-cycle

Fuel: Gasoline vapor

Ignition: Electric with make-and-break igniter

Number of Cylinders: 1

Bore x Stroke: 6" x 8"

HP @ RPM: 3 @ 250

Weight: 1,016 lbs.

Dimensions: 38" flywheel

Original Application: Unknown. Discovered in Canada on Victoria Island in poor condition and needing rod and main bearings, throttle valve, and rocker arm.

The potential for a brilliant inventor to be undone by the patent controversies that swirled throughout the whole pioneer period of internal combustion development was realized many times over. The most famous case of all involved Nicolaus Otto's loss of his famous German patent number 532 in January, 1886. Deeply humiliated by the event, Otto took solace in the fact that none of the many eminent engineers and attorneys with whom he spoke ever questioned his own personal integrity. Still, he never really got over the whole affair. Otto died five years later on January 26, 1891, at just 58 years of age.

At the time of Otto's death, and a world removed from European engine developments and conflicts, a 36 year-old engineer in San Francisco was involved in patent litigation of his own. The engineer's name was Daniel S. Regan. By this time, Regan had developed and then sold commercially in (1884 or 1885) his first Regan Vapor Engine. ("Vapor" referred to the gasoline vapors piped to the engine from a so-called carburetor or "oil tank.") This was a startling achievement by a man about whom little has been recorded. In November, 1893, the *San Francisco Call* described Regan as a San Francisco native and a "mechanical engineer with a well-developed taste for experimenting with the laws of motion [and] eighteen patents have been issued to him . . . ."

One of Regan's patents was granted in June 1885 for a make-and-break electric ignition system, "a certain device for igniting the charge of gas whereby the gas jet

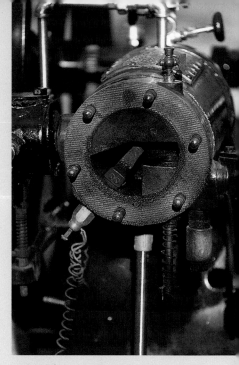

Below left is Daniel Regan's "electrical igniter for gas-engines, the combination, with a gas-chamber, of an insulated stud, a pivoted lever, said stud and lever being normally in circuit, and a finger carried by the piston-head and adapted to break the contact of the stud and lever, substantially as set forth." Above is the actual engine with cylinder head removed.

is dispensed with and the necessity of the slide valve is entirely avoided."

Daniel Regan was not the only man to conceive and patent a mechanical device that would, when its points were separated, create a spark that could ignite a fuel air mixture. But he certainly did apply the principle to a compression engine at an early date. The 1891 catalog listed nine upright and horizontal models of 3/4 to 15 horse-power, the latter a 2,300 pound double-cylinder engine.

From the distance of over a century in time, and in the absence of specific records, one can only assume that it was Regan's need for capital that led him to sell or assign part interests in his patents. The seeds for Regan's problems were sown almost immediately (in 1886) because some of his patents were jointly held, and the West Coast rights were assigned to one W. T. Garratt. Thus began what became a convoluted and ongoing assigning of patents, some of which, including Garratt's, were reassigned to other parties. One of the latter was Mora M. Barrett who was to become one of the organizers of the Pacific Gas Engine Company in San Francisco in 1890.

Although vindicated in an 1892 Appeals Court ruling, Daniel Regan was unable to reestablish himself. He formed the California Vapor Engine Company in 1892 but could not make it work. What became of Daniel S. Regan after 1893 is unknown. Industry insiders at Union sometimes referred to him as the "poor fellow" who really founded the gasoline engine business on the West Coast. Today, Regan engines are rare but a few remain and, much coveted by collectors, these treasures are the sole tangible evidence that Daniel S. Regan ever lived.

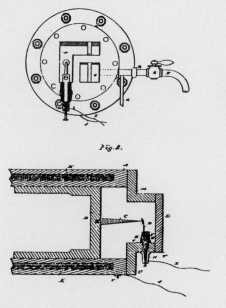

Fig. 2.

Regan's patented igniter

"Over 200 in Actual Operation"

PACIFIC

On May 15th, 1886, inventor Daniel S. Regan entered an agreement with W. T. Garratt that seemingly gave Garratt the Pacifc Coast license for "all such inventions and improvements, whether patented or not, which may be hereafter made by either of us in gas engines and the mechanism by which they are operated." Not quite three years later, in December, 1889, Garratt assigned his rights in the agreement (whatever they really were) to Mora M. Barrett who incorporated the Pacific Gas Engine Company on Fremont Street in San Francisco on April 22, 1890.

Barrett was listed as "manager" of the new company and William G. Barrett, perhaps Mora's father or a brother, was listed as president. The Pacific engine looks at first glance to be a pure copy of the vertical Regan and ads showing the vaporizer on the engine's right and the battery on its left only heighten the similarity. Description of the function of the vaporizing "carburetor" were essentially identical to those used by Regan. None of this should be surprising given that the Barretts obviously believed they had every right to use Regan's patented developments. To these, however, several innovations of Mora Barrett's were added. In particular, the exhaust valve mechanism of the Pacific is distinct.

Pacific got off to a strong start. The brochure published in 1891 contains a two page "List of Parties" giving the names of purchasers, their location, the horsepower of their engine and its application. The greatest number of Pacifics, mostly two- to four-horsepower models, were employed in pumping. But others were purchased to drive printing presses, generate electricity or drive launches.

Nearly all these engines were sold to California customers, but one went to Guatamala and another, to power a "street motor," went to Sydney, Australia. The Barretts invited prospects to compare the engine with anything else and stressed the superior materials and workmanship they offered "under the personal supervision of the patentees, themselves skilled mechanics."

Owner: Anton Affentranger
Manufacturer: Pacific Gas Engine Company
Year of Manufacture: Circa 1891
Place of Manufacture: San Francisco, California
Type: 4-cycle
Fuel: Gasoline
Ignition: Low-tension, piston-tripped ignitor
Number of Cylinders: 1
Bore x Stroke: 6" x 7"
HP @ RPM: 2
Dimensions: 34" flywheel. 45" high x 25" wide
Original Application: Found on a ranch west of
   Salinas Valley

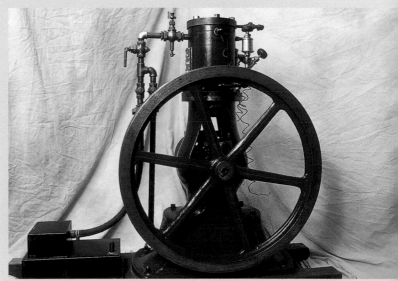

This claim did not hold true for long, apparently, as an article from the magazine *Industry* noted that "the company being unable to fill their orders have been compelled to contract for the construction of a number of engines to be made in other works…"

In July, 1891, Pacific won its first legal battle with Daniel Regan. One can assume feelings were bitter on all sides. A Pacific ad of that year notes that "We Have For Sale Cheap, Four Second-hand REGAN VAPOR ENGINES." Six months later, the court decision was reversed. In January, 1892, the Ninth Circuit Court of Appeals (Regan Vapor Engine Company vs. Pacific Gas Engine Company) overruled the previous decision and basically said that Regan did, in fact, still own his patents and that no rights were legally transferred to Pacific's Barrett. Still, it was a great mess and resulted in the undoing of both companies although Pacific did get the best of it (See Union.).

Pacific claimed to have sold 200 engines in 1891, but how many engines were built in total is unknown and survivors are extremely rare. The beautiful engine displayed here was found on a ranch in the central coast region of California. Its parts were scattered over a wide area. Each one was carefully gathered by collector John Richardson who methodically restored this most interesting example of the first epoch of commercial engine manufacture in California. It stands today as a testament to mechanical ingenuity that was foiled by the patent-related battles that could, at times, dominate the internal combustion engine business during the late 19th century.

Here is the two-cylinder version of what the Pacific Gas Engine Company called "the simplest and most efficient engine in the world." This "double" or "duplex" produced 15 horsepower. Pacifics like this were used in applications as diverse as driving a furnace blower at a foundry in Eureka, California, and for powering a schooner berthed at Florence, Oregon. The engine was rated for 200 rpm and weighed 3000 pounds. Its list price in 1891 was a significant $1,250.

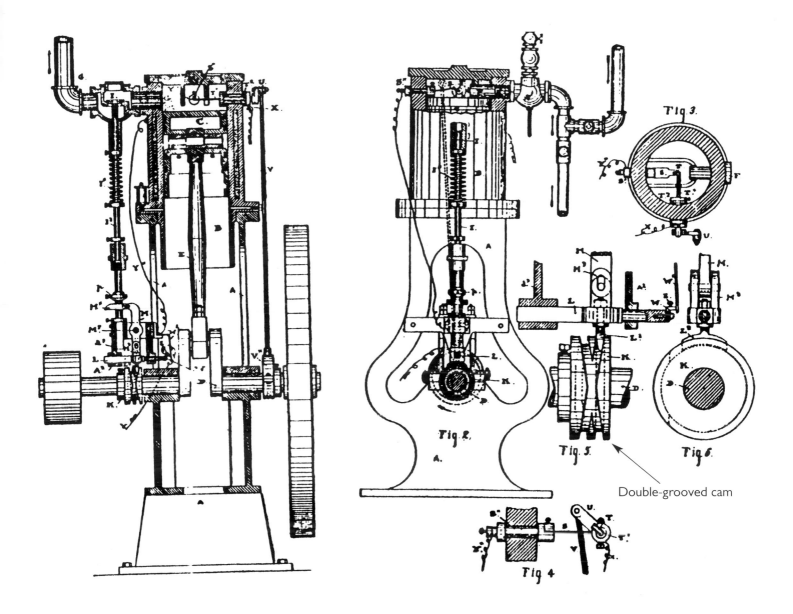

Double-grooved cam

How the Pacific Worked

The vapor is produced when air is drawn over gasoline in the "carburetor." This rich mixture passes into the inlet pipe on the engine where it is drawn into the cylinder through an atmospheric inlet valve on the piston's downstroke. Once the engine has started, the mixture is leaned and fine-tuned using a lever that permits pure air to enter the inlet pipe. This air is drawn from the base, which it enters through numerous holes, the goal being to provide a source of largely dust free air to the engine. As on the Regan, a projection on the piston moves the electrodes apart to create the ignition spark. The contacts are wired in series with a battery and low-tension coil.

The Pacific operates without gears. The exhaust valve is operated by a cam follower whose movement is dictated by a pattern of grooves on the crankshaft. The grooves of this ingenious "double grooved cam" as it was then known, crossed in one area. This caused the follower to lift and open the valve on one revolution and then move away from the cam on the next so as not to open the exhaust valve. With the engine running and the mixture correct, speed is adjusted by the "throttle" upstream of the two inlet levers.

DANIEL BEST

The Best wipe-spark igniter

Owner: Frank "Fergie" Ferguson
Manufacturer: The Daniel Best Manufacturing Company
Year of Manufacture: 1892
Place of Manufacture: San Leandro, California
Type: 4-cycle
Fuel: Gasoline
Ignition: Low-tension "wipe spark"
Number of Cylinders: 1
Bore x Stroke: 6" x 8"
HP @ RPM: 3 @ 240
Weight: 1050 lbs.
Dimensions: 58" long x 42 1/2" high
Original Application: Unknown. Had been used for pumping water on a sheep ranch.

How the Best Worked

Much of the mechanical fascination of the engine resides in its method of timing the "wipe spark" igniter. This term referred to flat, spring-type contacts 3/8 inches wide on each electrode. One of these springs remained stationary while the other was sprung in and out of contact by a lever timed to the crankshaft's rotation. The lever was operated by a wooden shaft driven by a cam fitted on the timing gear. Wood was necessary to isolate the hot electrode from the rest of the engine. The igniter's movable spring was said to last four to six months longer than some other types of make-and-break igniter points.

The machine shown here may be the only internal combustion engine ever designed by a man who once who traveled west with a wagon train, who fought for his life against indians, who lost several fortunes but died a millionaire, and who wound up being remembered as perhaps the most important figure in the history of a city. All this and more is true of Daniel Best who was born in Crawford County, Ohio, in 1838 and whose life was lived apparently without fear on the scale of a Hollywood epic.

By the time he was 28 years old, Daniel Best had acquired years of experience in farming, logging, and gold mining but, in 1868, he lost the first three fingers of his left hand to a circular saw in a mill near Olympia, Washington. Best then moved to Sutter County, California, where his brother Henry owned a ranch and it was this move that set the course for the rest of his life. During the winter of 1869 – '70, Best designed a portable grain cleaner and separator that freed farmers from carting their grain to a distant mill and paying someone else to process it. The result was a lucrative manufacturing business and the beginning of an inventing career that ultimately resulted in 41 patents. In 1888, he patented a combined steam traction engine and harvester/thresher that would prove hugely profitable. That year, too, he began experiments with gasoline engines and, two years later, applied for the first of 11 patents he was to receive on them.

By now, Best had settled in San Leandro where his dynamic business was the town's major employer and Best a leading citizen. His internal combustion engine was awarded a first place at the 1891 California State Fair and he soon adapted it to drive a "gasoline streetcar" in San Leandro. Another car in San Jose and a third operated on four miles of track linking Yuba City and Marysville. From the beginning, Best traded on his considerable reputation for integrity and brilliance.

Daniel Best (right) with his son, Leo, who would become chairman of Caterpillar. (Courtesy of San Leandro Public Library)

The engine was always referred to as "the Daniel Best" engine and the brochure noted that its manufacture was "under the personal supervision of Mr. Best, the patentee." At an early date, Best recognized the desirability of an engine that would operate on a variety of fuels. He designed an "improved gas generator" that would vaporize crude petroleum, distillate, or kerosene so that the engine would operate on those fuels as well as city gas and gasoline.

The engine pictured here dates to what was probably the very first year of Best engine production, 1892. It was discovered, mostly buried, on a northern California sheep ranch near Butte City in the 1970s and was subsequently completely restored. Among the unusual features of Best's engine was its one-piece base and block casting, which must have involved some artful casting and resulted in an exceptionally simple, sturdy foundation. Right from the start, Best was a proponent of electric ignition noting that there "is nothing more certain and inexpensive than the electric spark." Hot tube ignition was offered if customers preferred it.

Daniel Best retired from manufacturing in 1908 when he was 70 years old, selling his interests to the competing Holt Manufacturing Company. Daniel's son Leo retained his ownership shares, while in 1910 starting the C. L. Best Gas Traction Co. to build tracked tractors or "crawlers." Fifteen years later, Best and Holt merged to form the Caterpillar Tractor Company with Leo Best as chairman. As for Daniel, in retirement he was often seen driving the streets of San Leandro in a big Packard and overseeing construction of the Best Building, which still stands as a fine memento to a man who, virtually everyone agreed, was one of a kind.

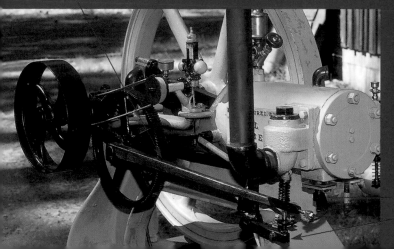

Wipe spark operating lever

Eccentric for moveable electrode

Eccentric for exhaust valve

A Stroke of Genius from Baltimore

WHITE & MIDDLETON

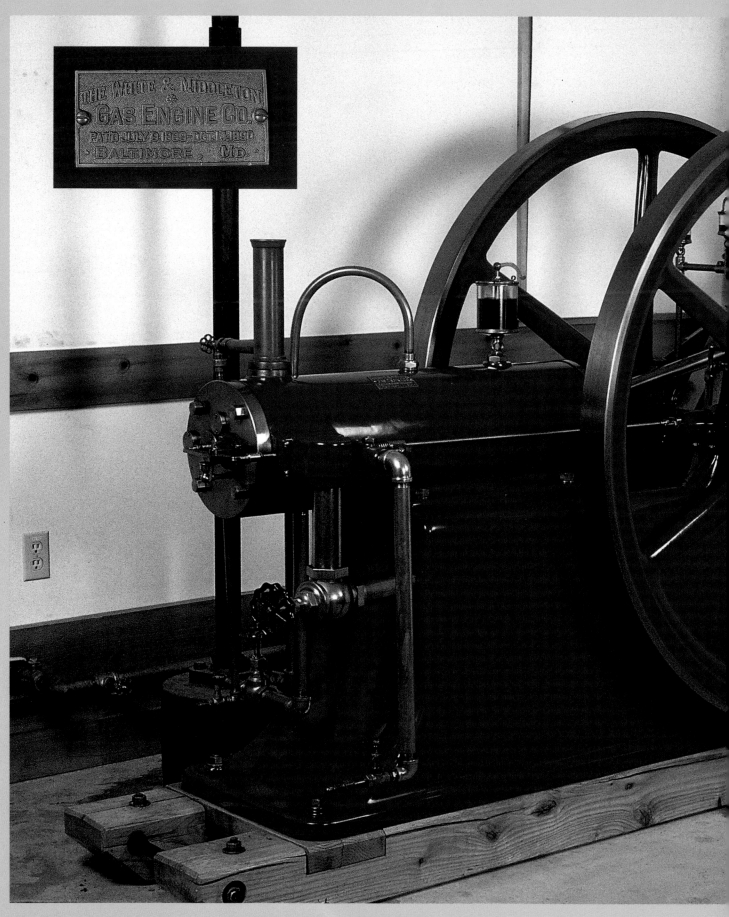

The men who made the greatest impact during the early days of the internal combustion century combined a unique gift for mechanics, a seemingly innate understanding of the new technology with which they were dealing, adequate capital and good business sense. When all these qualities were combined, a quite robust business could result. That is what happened in the case of two Baltimore machinists named Arthur Middleton and Charles White. The pair met as young men while employed at the Detrich & Harvey Machine Company in 1876 and eventually, in 1889, applied jointly for a patent on a gas engine. Patents for improved versions followed in 1890, 1894, and 1895.

These patents were the basis for the White & Middleton Gas Engine Company, which was established in Baltimore at Pratt Street and East Falls Avenue. Working in a field often characterized by great originality and cleverness, White and Middleton developed an engine that was quickly recognized for its ingenious simplicity. The method developed for getting mixture into the engine and out of it was extraordinary, and the patented governor contributed to extremely steady running ("as steady as any steam engine") making the engine popular for electric lighting purposes, among other things. The engine's long stroke — over twice the bore dimension — lessened the angle at which the connecting rod worked, reducing the tendency of the back end to lift and "walk." It also made for a long service life. One of the engines was known to have been run 16-18 hours a day powering line-shafts for 40 years without major service.

Owner: Mary Ellen Susong
Manufacturer: White & Middleton Gas Engine Company
Year of Manufacture: October 25, 1893
Place of Manufacture: Baltimore, Maryland
Type: 4-cycle
Fuel: Natural Gas
Ignition: Hot Tube
Number of Cylinders: 1
Bore x Stroke: 6 1/2" x 16"
HP: 10
Weight: 3100 pounds
Dimensions: 7' 2" long x 2' 8" wide
Original Application: Provided power at a state hospital in Indiana.

The engine line grew quickly in both model offerings and sales. White and Middleton soon moved to larger quarters on Charles and Winder Streets and began building stationary and marine engines of from one to eight cylinders. By 1898, it was reported that 300 of the engines were in use in Baltimore with another 1,000 in various locations throughout the country. Bell Telephone was a major customer and owned some 300 White & Middleton engines for use as stand-by power.

All this happened to coincide with the work of another inventive genius in town named Simon Lake. His interest was submarines. In 1897, Lake built a 36'9" submersible boat named *Argonaut* powered by a 30-horsepower gasoline engine built by White & Middleton. The boat was said to have been the first submarine to navigate in open water. A bigger boat built by Lake in 1901 was powered by a pair of White & Middleton engines.

Arthur Middleton and Edward White had a falling out some time in 1910 when White was granted a patent relating to burning heavy oil in two- and four-cycle engines on which both men had worked. That

Arthur Middleton (1862–1933). (Courtesy of Edward L. Middleton)

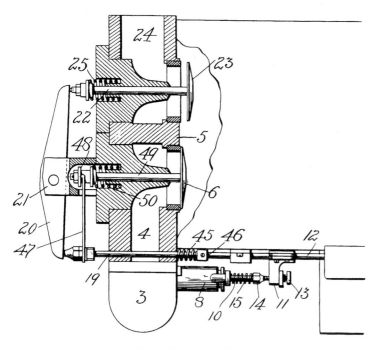

Detail of the White & Middleton cylinder head of 1904. The design was developed to provide steadier running than a typical engine after the gas flow had been cut off by the governor which, the patent said, allowed "the conditions of temperature and moisture within the combustion chamber to become abnormal." The solution, in this case, was a small fuel pump (8) that worked in conjunction with the governor and inlet valve #6. While the inlet valve was held closed during the period when fuel was cut off, the little pump provided a small, initial charge of fuel that supplemented the normal mixture once the governor permitted the inlet to again open. Said the White & Middleton patent, "This excess or initial charge compensates for the changed conditions in the explosion chamber arising from the want of charges fed thereto with regularity."

November, White & Middleton was sold to the Bartlett Hayward Company and, subsequently, to Koppers Company, which ceased production in 1925, and ultimately sold the rights and drawings to the engines. Of the two partners, it is known that Arthur Middleton and his brother started the Middleton, Means Gas Engine Company in Baltimore in 1911 and that Middleton invented a watertight propeller shaft bearing in 1917. Arthur Middleton's son Edward, who researched his talented father, reported that Gottlieb Daimler visited the White & Middleton factory, probably during his 1893 trip to America to attend the Columbian Exposition in Chicago. Daimler is said to have considered Middleton a "genius." Later, a top executive of Fairbanks-Morse told Edward that the company had once considered White & Middleton to be among its toughest competitors. Arthur Middleton died at age 71 in 1933.

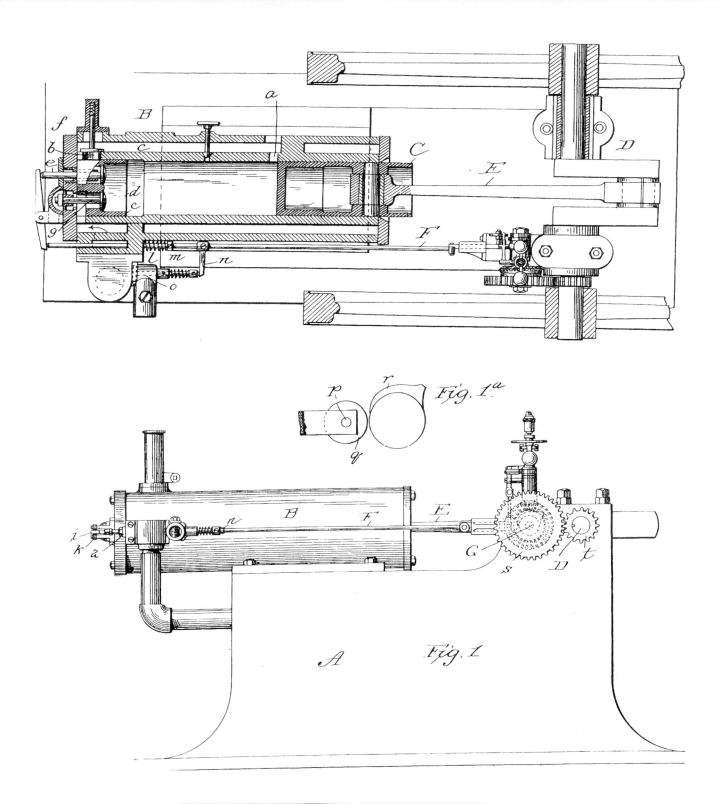

Fig. 1ª

Fig. 1

How the White and Middleton Worked

While air entered the cylinder through a conventional atmospheric intake valve, the method of exhaust was unique. In addition to a pushrod-actuated exhaust valve, there were also exhaust ports in the cylinder wall. These tended to relieve the engine of burnt gas and heat sooner that relying on the traditional method. The exhaust valve itself served to fully cleanse the cylinder of exhaust gases on the engine's exhaust stroke. Straight-cut gears on the crankshaft drove the vertical governor. "We have found that locating the governing mechanism on a shaft parallel to the crank-shaft and rotated therefrom enables us to secure compactness, stability, and great efficiency with the least number of parts and by the particular construction to provide for the most sensitive action of the governing mechanism," read the 1895 patent.

REID

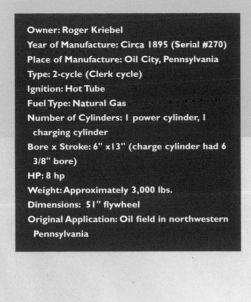

Owner: Roger Kriebel
Year of Manufacture: Circa 1895 (Serial #270)
Place of Manufacture: Oil City, Pennsylvania
Type: 2-cycle (Clerk cycle)
Ignition: Hot Tube
Fuel Type: Natural Gas
Number of Cylinders: 1 power cylinder, 1 charging cylinder
Bore x Stroke: 6" x13" (charge cylinder had 6 3/8" bore)
HP: 8 hp
Weight: Approximately 3,000 lbs.
Dimensions: 51" flywheel
Original Application: Oil field in northwestern Pennsylvania

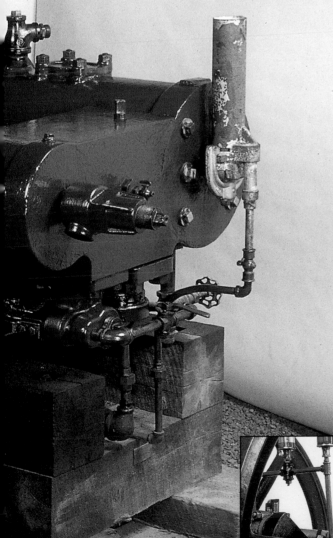

The Reid's charging cylinder delivered the air/gas mixture to the power cylinder.

On August 27th, 1859, a persistent ex-Railway Express agent and train conductor named Edwin L. Drake, and a drilling specialist named Billy Smith succeeded in their effort to find an oil source beneath the gravel and shale of a western Pennsylvania waterway called Oil Creek. The eventual success of an effort that some locals had referred to as Drake's Folly was abetted by a steam engine which, although it once caught fire, was in large part responsible for boring the 69 1/2-foot hole that became the world's first oil well. There, in the steep and wooded hills near Titusville, Pennsylvania, was born the industry that eventually would fuel the great rise of internal combustion.

During the subsequent three decades, and in the years that followed, the limitations of steam power in the country's expanding oil fields became obvious. A separate engine and boiler were needed for each well. Coal was expensive, and using natural gas was inefficient. Of course, time was consumed merely in getting up steam pressure to begin operation. These difficulties were seized on as opportunities by those who understood the potential of the internal combustion engine. The first of those who thought to apply internal combustion to the oil fields did so in the pioneer period of the movement and one of the earliest and most successful was a Scottish-born immigrant who, among other things, had a small "oil production" himself near Oil City, Pennsylvania. His name was Joseph Reid.

Born in November, 1843, in Maybole, Scotland, Reid's formative years were typical of many who devoted themselves to the new art and science of internal combustion engines. His formal schooling ended at age 11 after which he was apprenticed as a joiner for four years. With his desire to learn engineering, Reid then turned, as did so many others, to the dominant industry in England for training. He became a machinist for the Glasgow and Southwestern Railroad Company. He remained in Scotland until 1862 and then began the familiar path followed by so many in his vocation.

Joseph Reid pursued his trade in North America, first in Montreal, then in New York, Boston, Wilmington, Delaware, and Cumberland, Maryland. He

Joseph Reid received a patent on his two-cycle engine in 1898. (Courtesy of Margaret Reid)

reached Pennsylvania, finally, by securing a job with the Baldwin Locomotive Works, the prosperous steam engine builder in Philadelphia, where he remained until 1876. Reid went on to work for two more companies before setting up a general machine shop in Western Pennsylvania where he soon became intimately familiar with all the esoteric equipment used in the oil fields. He developed a line of refinery equipment and, with the opening of new oil fields in Lima, Ohio, he developed an oil burner that was the basis in 1885 of the Reid Burner Company.

During much of this period, apparently, Joseph Reid was thinking about the limitations that steam power represented for oil men. It was a time during which all the periodicals that would be read by men such as Reid — *The American Machinist, The Scientific American,* and others — were recounting the latest news of the internal combustion pioneers. At some point in the period between 1886 and 1894, Joseph Reid began planning an engine of his own. Initially, the design was one intended to operate on crude oil but it was during the engine's development that Reid happened upon a most elegant idea. Since natural gas was a by-product of oil field operations, why not simply run the engine off this potential fuel?

That is exactly the sort of engine Reid came up with. He sold his first engine in 1894, apparently as an adjunct to the Reid Burner Company's offerings. Then, in 1899, the growing engine business led to the formation of the Joseph Reid Gas Engine Company, which soon grew to occupy a large parcel along the banks of the Allegheny River in Oil City. A decade later, Reid gas engines were pumping away in oil fields throughout the United States, in Mexico, and as far away as India.

Exactly how Joseph Reid developed his engine is now murky. In a brief retrospective on the company's early days published in 1934, it was reported that Reid "was acquainted with some of the work which had been done in England on the development of a two-cycle engine. . . . He accordingly set out to overcome the two difficulties which had prevented the success of the two-cycle engine, namely, ignition and governing."

The engine shown here is a prime example of Reid's first-generation design. What it reflects most dramatically is "some of the work which had been done in England on the development of a two-cycle engine." The architecture of this Reid follows that of

How the Reid Worked

Gas and air is drawn through the throttle mixer and upward through a spring-loaded valve into the charging cylinder, which is timed to run 90 degrees ahead of the power cylinder. When the power piston uncovers the exhaust port near the bottom of its stroke, a one-way valve connecting the charging cylinder and power cylinder is forced open, admitting the fuel mixture and helping to expel the burnt gases from the power cylinder. The piston now compresses the mixture, which is ignited by the hot tube. A "pop-off" valve in the charging cylinder opens in the case of "crossfires."

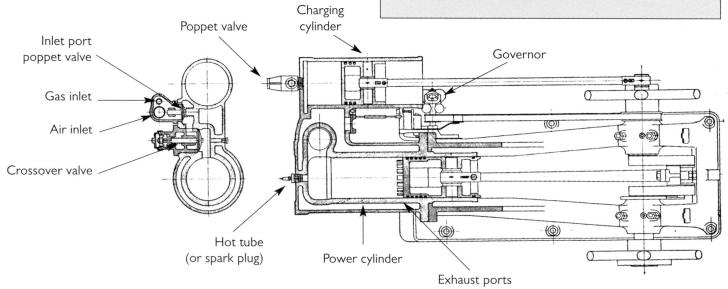

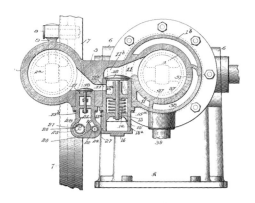

the engine developed by Reid's fellow Scotsman, Dugald Clerk. Born in Glasgow in 1854 and formally educated in science, Clerk made a careful study of the internal combustion engine developed in the United States in 1872 by the Rhode Island-born George B. Brayton. The Brayton possessed a separate "charging cylinder" that compressed and transferred the air/gas mixture to a "power cylinder." Flame ignition exploded the mixture on each full revolution of the crankshaft, hence the two-stroke designation.

By 1881, Clerk had developed a two-cycle engine with a compressor cylinder and working cylinder that worked on the two-cycle principle (referred to in England, at least, as the Clerk cycle) with reliable ignition based on open flame and a slide valve. The advantage of the two-cylinder configuration was that it permitted timely and improved "scavenging" or displacement of the burned exhaust gas by the in-rushing mixture. The mixture was then compressed and ignited. This engine was introduced in the United States in 1882 by the Clerk Gas Engine Company, which had its headquarters in Philadelphia. The engine was not a commercial success.

The engine developed by Joseph Reid reflected the basics of Clerk's work although Reid was granted his own patent for a two-cycle engine "with pump and adjacent cylinder" in 1898. On the Reid, a flywheel-driven connecting rod pinned to a flywheel spoke operated the charging cylinder mounted next to the power cylinder. Ignition was by hot tube. Flyweights on the governor operated spool-type valves to control the amount of mixture admitted to the power cylinder. The engine was notable both for greater fuel efficiency than a typical, port-controlled two-cycle, and for very high torque.

Unlike the Clerk engine, Reid's was an immediate commercial success. Not only did the engine operate powerfully and reliably on the abundant natural gas of the oil fields, but Reid envisioned the engine as the centerpiece of a "system" that would give oil men exactly what they required. In 1899, he patented a reversing clutch which, mounted on the flywheel hub, allowed the engine to drive equipment in two directions, a necessity for drilling or cleaning out wells. This was followed by manufacture of an "eccentric power." It was this device — a horizontally mounted wheel — that transferred power from the engine to the many wells it operated through the ingenious "rod lines" that snaked their fascinating trails all across an "oil lease" turning corners, ascending and descending hills, even going underground or airborne over a road as necessary.

One such arrangement owned by the Preston Oil Machinery Company was described as follows: "The 8 hp engine was installed about December 2, 1901. . . . It now operates 13 wells having an average depth of 460 feet. It is a little over 1200 feet from the power house [location of the engine and the 'power'] to the farthest well." The Preston's engine was in continuous operation for some 13 years before it was replaced.

By the early 1900s, Joseph Reid's products were an integral part of the oil field business and the plant was steadily expanded. After a devastating fire in December, 1918 — caused by a steam locomotive engineer who refused to halt his train until an oil leak from the Reid factory that had flooded the tracks was cleaned up — the company was revitalized. New engine models were introduced featuring roller bearings. Leadership of the firm remained in the family for Joseph Reid's nephew John took over as president and was also known widely throughout the oil equipment industry. In 1928, he became a director of the American Petroleum Institute. The company ceased production in 1939, although parts operations continued until 1955.

A Peculiar Marvel
SPRINGFIELD

How the Springfield Worked

The Springfield is nothing if not highly original. The engine's side shaft drives an "overhead" camshaft that operates the intake and exhaust valves, igniter, and fuel pump. The fuel system is unusual. Fuel is admitted to the fuel pump by a plunger-driven valve actuated by the camshaft. The fuel is then "injected" under pressure into the air pipe leading to the cylinder by the pump's second plunger. The stroke of the latter plunger is adjustable to control the mixture ratio. Said the instruction manual: "If it fires back out the air pipe, turn on a little more. If the exhaust is smoky, decrease the amount." A belt-driven "hit-and-miss" fly-weight governor disconnects the fuel pump plunger cam to maintain speed. Said the manual:

"The engines are sent from the factory properly speeded."

In addition to the "normal" intake and exhaust valve, the engine also has a secondary inlet valve. The air/fuel mixture entering the holding chamber from the air pipe reaches this chamber, which is upstream from the auxiliary intake valve, before passing through the valve and into a passage that connects with the actual intake valve. The valves open simultaneously. The holding chamber was intended to promote improved vaporization of the mixture although Tom Stockton, the engine's owner and a highly capable engineer, believes there is little functional benefit either to it or the dual intake valves.

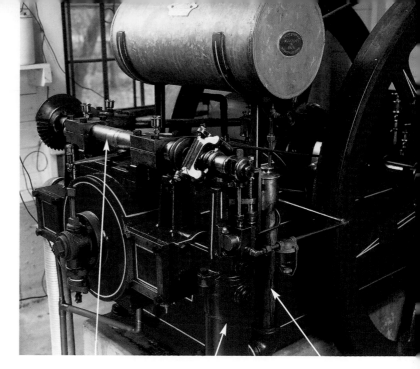

The Springfield Gas Engine Company was incorporated on New Year's Day 1892. Hopes were no doubt high for Peter Coffield, the president, and Charles Paxson, the vice president. Although the two had patented a vertical engine two years earlier, the company they now formed would build a series of horizontal engines of from one- to 25 horsepower, all with electric ignition. The Springfield is a "headless" design, meaning a single casting sufficed for the cylinder and head, eliminating the head gasket. Big valve chests are bolted to either side of the cylinder and an igniter chamber plate is mounted atop the cylinder.

By 1893, a new 40' x 125' foot two-story factory was in operation and engines were being shipped out of Springfield to, the owners reported, "distant sections of the country." Then, as was often the case with start-up engine companies, disagreements — almost always well camouflaged from the public and from the historical record — arose between the partners. At the Gas Engine Company in Springfield in 1890, for example, Clark Sintz split from his partner John Foos to go his own way. In 1896, Charles Paxson left the Springfield Gas Engine Company for greener pastures in Dayton and another start-up, Callahan.

Springfield continued on, of course, and developed an apparently profitable business for a time. By 1901, it

Cam shaft   Holding chamber   Air pipe

was reporting sales to England and Cuba as well as domestically. A dozen years after the company's founding, Springfield set forth its strategy quite simply as the production of "a strictly high-grade engine. We do not attempt to compete in price with many builders." It may not have been a strategy contrived to ensure long-term survival but it did produce some most interesting engines including the one pictured here.

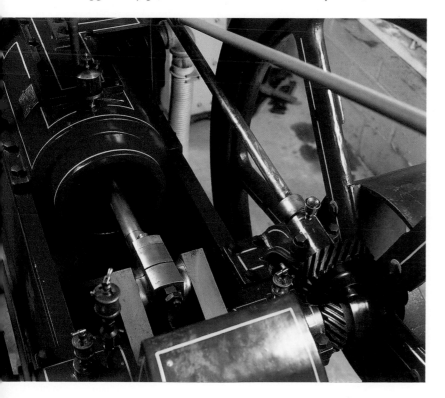

Owner: Tom Stockton

Year of Manufacture: 1896

Place of Manufacture: Springfield, Ohio

Type: 4-cycle

Fuel: Gasoline

Ignition: Make-and-break igniter using Edison caustic batteries

Number of Cylinders: 1

Bore x Stroke: 9" x 12"

HP @ RPM: 10 @ 170

Weight: 8,500 lbs.

Dimensions: 57" flywheels, 3 1/2-feet wide

Original Application: Powered a cider mill near Waterloo, Michigan.

The German Immigrants' Engine
CHARTER

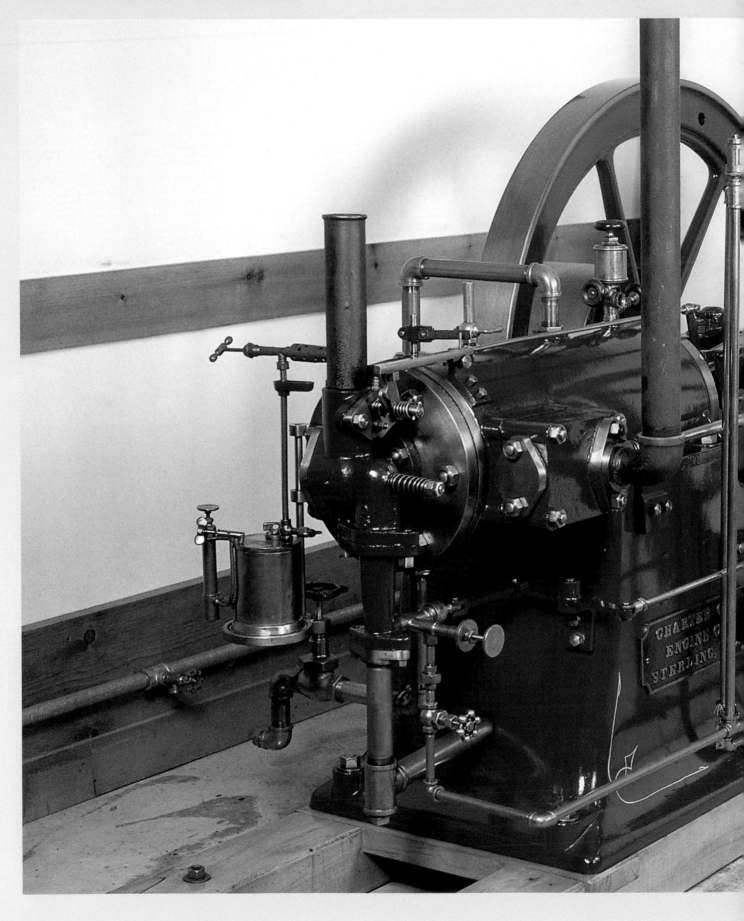

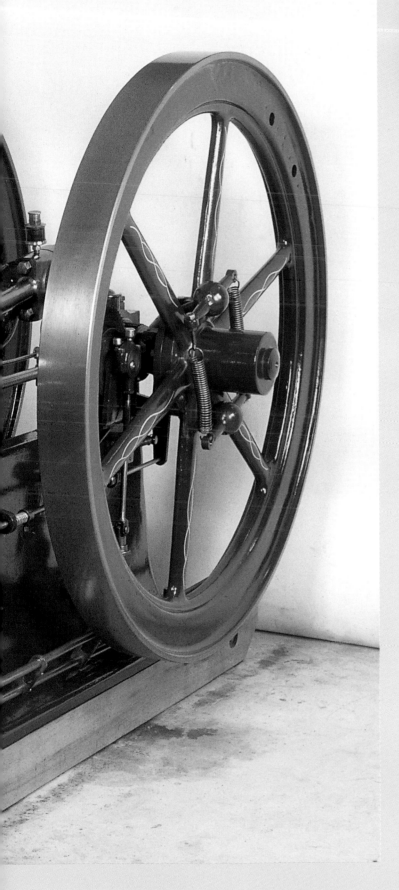

The story of internal combustion engine development in America is chock-full of claims about being the first to do something. In May, 1931, the *Sterling Daily Gazette* of Sterling, Illinois, entered the claims game by proclaiming: "The first application of gasoline for power purposes in the history of mankind resulted from the experiments conducted by Frank Burger, a mechanical engineer engaged by the Williams and Orton Co., afterward the Charter Gas Engine Co., of Sterling, which culminated in his solution of the problem in 1886, when the first gasoline engine the world ever knew began running and continued to run as long as gasoline was supplied."

When considering this claim, one immediately must think of Daniel Regan's vapor engine, which predated Burger's by as many as three years, and of Daimler and Maybach. There is no doubt, however, that the Charter engine built in Sterling, Illinois, was among the earliest internal combustion engines to employ gasoline in liquid form rather vapor as a fuel. As it happened, this very feature became the source of serious conflict between the two men who had joined together to enter the engine business, and the story of the Charter

Owner: **Mary Ellen Susong**
Manufacturer: **Charter Gas Engine Company**
Year of Manufacture: **Circa 1897 (Serial #1387)**
Place of Manufacture: **Sterling, Illinois**
Type: **4-cycle**
Fuel: **Gasoline**
Ignition: **Make-and-break or hot tube (gasoline-fired)**
Number of Cylinders: **1**
Bore x Stroke: **8 3/8" " x 13"**
HP: **12**
Original Application: **Said to have run a cider press in New England**

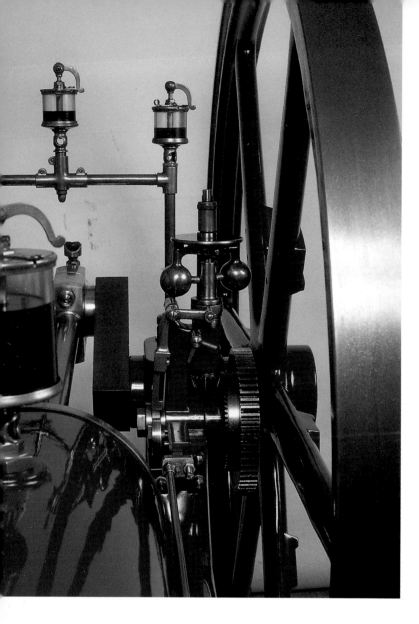

Orton machinery manufacturing company, told his workmen, "Boys, that kind of a machine will be our future business." It was a moment nobody present ever forgot.

While he understood machinery, John Charter was a cigar maker by training and if he were going to enter engine manufacture, he would need an engine man. It was while on a trip to Washington in 1880 to investigate likely-looking patents that he found Burger's. Charter convinced Burger to leave his model-making shop and resettle in Sterling, which Burger did, most likely in 1880. Initially he developed a two-cycle gas engine with a separate charging cylinder, an engine that would not be subject to a patent lawsuit from the Philadelphia builders of the Otto. Although the engine was Burger's, the patent (and several subsequent ones) was registered in 1883 in John Charter's name. Years later, some newspaper accounts would incorrectly ascribe to Charter the engine's creation.

In addition to his important position at the Williams & Orton Company, John Charter was also president of the local gas company. He foresaw that he could profit not only from engine building but from increased use of gas itself, and it was this motive that helped lead to conflict with Franz Burger. With the initial Charter model behind him, Burger focused on the realization of his liquid fuel engine, and a Charter patent for the new machine was issued in 1887. A six-horsepower prototype model was sold to a local machine shop for $1,000 and successfully replaced the steam engine that had previously driven the machinery there. Key to Burger's engine was a so-called injector, a small pump and needle valve that dispensed liquid gasoline into the engine's air intake. That first engine worked in a satisfactory manner for the next six years until it was replaced by a 20-horsepower model.

According to the son of George Robinson, a

Engine Company is, like that of many early engine-building enterprises, a tangled web.

Franz Burger emigrated from Germany to America in the early 1870s and, by 1880, was a partner in a shop that produced the important and delightful patent models used to demonstrate new inventions. Mr. Burger was an inventor himself, and brought with him to America his great interest in internal combustion engines fostered initially perhaps by some familiarity with the Otto and Langen engine. In 1878, Burger received a patent for an engine that would operate on kerosene or gasoline. The engine was never built but Burger's work caught the attention of another German immigrant named John Charter.

Born in Germany in 1838, Charter emigrated with his parents and, at some point, he presumably either anglicized or changed his name. Charter's interest in internal combustion had been ignited by the Otto engine that he saw at the Philadelphia Exposition of 1876. Charter, who then presided over the Williams &

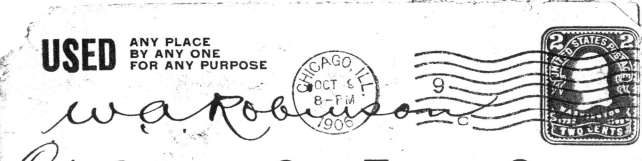

Williams & Orton director, John Charter resisted development of the gasoline engine in favor of a gas engine. The rather odd result of this was the removal of John Charter from Williams & Orton at the same time as it changed its name to the Charter Gas Engine Company in 1889. Like so many such episodes in the history of early engine makers, this was a nasty business. John Charter still had power as the patents were in his name. When the company sold rights for a version of the engine to the Keystone Manufacturing Company, which planned a portable version for agricultural markets, Charter attempted to intervene for the $10,000 involved.

In 1889 or 1890, John Charter and his son James moved to Chicago to establish a new engine company together with machinery maker H. W. Caldwell. The Caldwell-Charter engine developed by James was a promising engine but the business did not thrive. The rights to the engine and the patterns were sold to Charles Hosmer Morse and became the foundation of Fairbanks-Morse. James Charter was for a time the company's chief engineer. Back in Sterling, Franz Burger continued as engineer at Charter and, with the legal defeat of the Otto patent, a four-cycle Charter was developed. In 1893, Burger left Sterling for Fort Wayne, Indiana, where he consulted in engineering matters and, of course, continued to invent. He died in 1908. Burger's old partner John Charter died in 1901 at age 63, and was mourned as one of Sterling's leading citizens. As for Charter, it remained a pillar of the industry. In 1923, it bought out the old firm of Mietz and Weiss, pioneer of hot bulb engines, and moved it from New York to Sterling. By 1931, the company was producing engines of up to 200 horsepower in one of the most modern plants in the country. The survivor shown here is from the early days of Charter production and is the result of a total restoration.

The Great Idea
DIESEL

Of all the internal combustion pioneers, only one man was destined to be immortalized by having his name routinely applied to a type of engine. That man was Rudolf Diesel. Brilliant of mind, elegant in appearance and manner, Diesel was recognized by all who met him as a man of extraordinary gifts. As it turned out, the inventor would need every ounce of the brainpower, willpower, and physical stamina with which he was blessed to persevere through the trying years of work required to develop the engine that bears his name. In the end, the burdens Diesel faced would prove too much even for him.

Diesel was born in Paris in 1858, the son of a leather goods maker who, with his wife, had left Augsburg in Bavaria seeking greater business opportunities. The family lived in Paris until 1870 when anti-German sentiment during the Franco-Prussian war forced a move to London, where Diesel's mother Elise had once worked as a companion to an Englishwoman. Rudolf stayed with his parents only a couple of months before being sent to school in Augsburg. His memories of London's working poor and smoke-filled skies, and later his impressions of the working class in Germany, would lead him to write a book proposing the need for social welfare plans.

From Augsburg, a homesick Diesel sent letters to his parents. He was applying himself hard to his studies. "In Germany, one must learn," he wrote. He often studied until midnight. By 1872, he had decided to become an engineer. Eight years later, he graduated from Munich's Technical University with the highest marks since the school's opening 12 years before. He was much admired by the faculty and, years later, would find support from professors there for his engine. In January, 1893, with the support of his wife Martha, Rudolf Diesel published the theories he had developed for an internal combustion engine. The booklet was entitled *Theory and Construction of a Rational Heat Engine to Replace Steam Engines and the Currently Known Combustion Engines.*

Diesel's theories involved an engine that would compress air to such a degree that the heat generated would serve to cause the ignition of fuel introduced to the cylinder. The patent he received would be the basis for a substantial fortune made from licensing contracts, but it would also be the subject of ongoing legal disputes regarding its wording, its meaning, and the nature of its real claims.

The development of the engine itself was to challenge Diesel in every way: financially, physically, intellectually, and emotionally. The technical obstacles of how to inject fuel, of what sort of fuel to use (coal gas or kerosene), of whether compression alone would reliably ignite it, were only some of the more prominent hurdles. It required some four years from the time the first experimental machine was built in 1893 until the third and successful prototype was made in 1897. That is the engine pictured here. In 1905, the builder, the Maschinenfabrik Augsburg, whose director Heinrich von Buz had constructed the prototypes and then went on to manufacture the engine, presented it to the German Museum in Munich.

The diesel was first shown to the buying public at an engine exposition in Munich in the summer of 1898. License arrangements were made abroad, the earliest with Carels Freres (Carels Brothers) in Belgium, in France with Dyckhoff, with Mirrlees, Watson & Yaryan in Scotland, and with Adolphus Busch in the U.S. Diesel himself now acquired great wealth. He built a big villa in Munich and provided lavishly for his family. At the same time, he never escaped the enmity of those who challenged his patent and the manner in which he presented his theories. While he consulted, gave lectures, and pursued new developments, Diesel was unable to remain a central figure in the great industry that his engine had helped to found. He was also beset by health problems and then by devastating financial reverses. Rudolf Diesel drowned himself by jumping from a cross-channel steamer on its way to England on September 29, 1913.

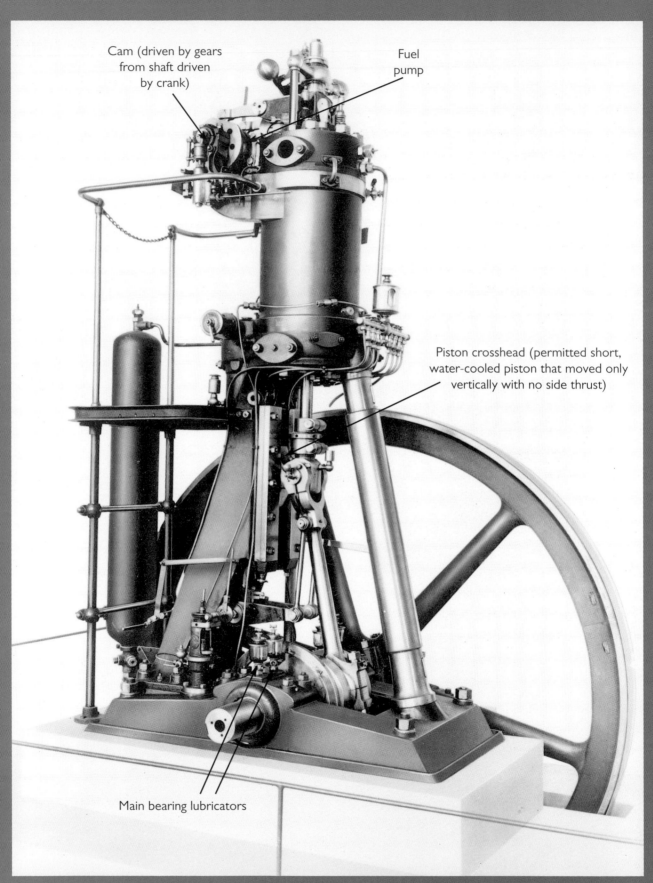

Cam (driven by gears from shaft driven by crank)

Fuel pump

Piston crosshead (permitted short, water-cooled piston that moved only vertically with no side thrust)

Main bearing lubricators

Rudolf Diesel's first successful diesel as tested February 17, 1897. Production models had a more conventional cast base rather than the tripod design. (Courtesy of MAN Nutzfahrzeuge Aktiengesellschaft, Nürnberg)

How the Diesel Worked

The engine's pedestal is a tripod consisting of the iron cylinder casting and a tubular support column. Compressed air from an integral tank was used both for starting and to atomize the fuel, which was injected at the needed pressure through an exhaustively developed plunger-style pump and spray nozzle. The injected fuel was ignited by the heat of the air compressed by the piston within the cylinder.

Diesel's patent number 67207 awarded by the Kaiser's Patent Office in Berlin on Feb. 28, 1892. (Courtesy of MAN Nutzfahrzeuge Aktiengesellschaft, Nürnberg)

Arm-in-arm are Rudolf Diesel, Heinrich von Buz, the visionary manager of Maschinenfabrik Augsburg, and Moritz Schröter of the Munich Technical University (Diesel's alma mater) who supported Diesel's theories and conducted the February 1897 testing of the third engine. (Courtesy of MAN Nutzfahrzeuge Aktiengesellschaft, Nürnberg)

OLDS

Owner: Nathan Lillibridge
Year of Manufacture: Circa 1898
Place of Manufacture: Lansing, Michigan
Type: 4-cycle
Fuel: Gasoline
Ignition: Hot Tube
Number of Cylinders: 1
HP @ RPM: 2 1/2 @ 300 - 350
Weight: 975 lbs.
Original Application: Unknown

In 1880, a blacksmith, machinist, and pattern maker named Pliny F. Olds moved with his family from Ohio to Lansing, Michigan where he established a shop to repair steam engines and farm machinery. A drawing of the period shows a sign on the roof that read Olds & Son. This soon became P. F. Olds and son, and the son referred to was Wallace Olds. In 1883, Wallace's 19-year-old younger brother Ransom joined the company, beginning a career that would see him become one of the country's most successful and influential automotive pioneers and manufacturers. Two years later, Ransom bought out his older brother's share and the company began a steady growth.

Steam power was good to the Olds family. Stationary and marine engines were responsible for increasing sales and Ransom Olds built his first steam-powered vehicle, a three-wheeler car in 1887. The company was incorporated in 1890 and Ransom continued his automotive experiments with a steam-powered four-wheel vehicle in 1890. By 1894, however, it must have been clear to Ransom Olds that internal combustion engines offered the best potential for the future, and he then began experimenting with them.

One can assume that Olds was so convinced about the potential of gasoline engines that he feared business would suffer in the absence of an Olds-built internal combustion engine. The result of this was the blatantly twisted wording of the company's 1894 brochure and press releases. "The Olds Gasoline Engine" read the headline in *The Scientific American* for June 9, 1894. "The Gasoline Engine Works" read the title of the P. F. Olds and Son catalog of that year. "We herewith give notice that we are the original inventors of the celebrated Gasoline Engines, and commenced manufacture of them in 1885," claimed the brochure's introduction. It was even replete with customer testimonials that expressed satisfaction with Olds "gasoline engines." But it was all a lie. The engines were steam engines equipped with gasoline-fired boilers.

In 1895, Ransom Olds together with a company engineer named Madison Bates filed for a patent on a vapor engine, and a year later Olds produced his first gasoline-powered car. By 1897, Olds had gathered the necessary investors and formed the Olds Motor Vehicle Company and that November, P. F. Olds & Son was reorganized to better reflect the product it would manufacture. It was now called the Olds Gasoline Engine Works. Based on subsequent events, one can conclude that Ransom had more interest in automotive design and making real his vision for mass production than in stationary engines.

The Olds Gasoline Engine Works was in full production of a "real" gasoline engine by 1897 and it must have reflected Madison Bates's and Ransom Olds's conception of a straightforward design that did away with the complexities of much of the competition. "It is built on the true engine principle, only two poppet valves operate direct from the main shaft. [Inaccurate as the intake valve was atmospheric] No complicated gear devices to oil and keep in repair," said the catalog. A testimonial written in 1899 by a Pennsylvania man who had owned his Olds engine for a year noted: "No gears or worm gears, cams, rock-arms, counter-shafts, levers etc, on the Olds engine to oil and keep in repair." In fact, the engine is known to many still as the "Gearless Olds." The engine featured a patented governor that permitted easy speed adjustment, a patented water pump, and hot tube ignition. The model line was comprehensive. The smallest engines were one horsepower and 2 1/2 horsepower verticals; the others were horizontal in layout ranging up to 50 horsepower. A widespread network of agents together with the engine's simple design and operation resulted in strong sales.

Ransom Olds's automotive career left little or no time for the stationary engine business but the latter's profitability prompted the two companies — the Engine Works and the Motor Vehicle Company — to be brought together in 1898. The firm was now known as the Olds Motor Works, Inc. It was during that same year that Ransom's brother Wallace, who was running the Engine Works was forced out by labor trouble. Eventually, in 1904, Ransom himself would, after profound disagreements with majority shareholders, leave the company that bore his name to found the very successful automotive firm, REO (Ransom E. Olds).

Over at what had been the Engine Works, Madison Bates left, probably in 1899, to form a new engine company in Lansing called Bates and Edmonds. Production of the Olds stationary engines continued on, however. At the St, Louis Exposition in 1904, an Olds engine could be seen generating electricity for a large restaurant and pavilion. The hot tube had given way to jump spark ignition. By this time, the company was known as the Olds Gas Power Company. Subsequently, the engines were produced by the Seager Engine Works and the Reliance Engineering Company. The engine shown here is from the earlier era of production and it still bears the paint decoration scheme shown in the catalog of 1899. The engine has the open crankcase familiar to steam practice but the base houses the fuel tank which, owners were cautioned, was not to be filled while the hot tube was burning.

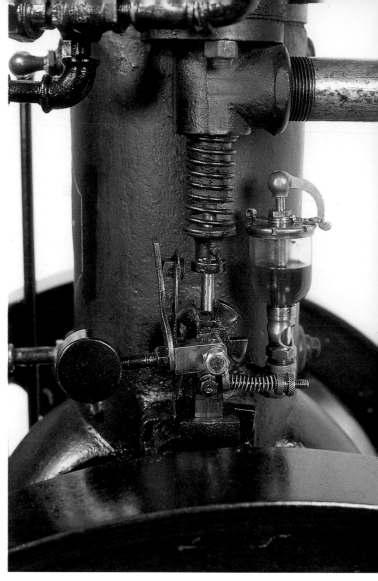

(Right) The ratchet wheel, which was indexed to the crankshaft, operated the exhaust valve and was one of the key components that made the Olds "gearless."

(Below) There's a lot going on atop the Olds cylinder head. Visible are the chimney for the hot tube, the spring and stem of the atmospheric inlet valve, and the fuel sight bowl. The brass "pressure dome" was intended to smooth fuel pressure fluctuations to the burner and act as a reservoir to help fire up the burner when initially starting the engine. The knob on the right controls fuel flow to the hot tube's burner.

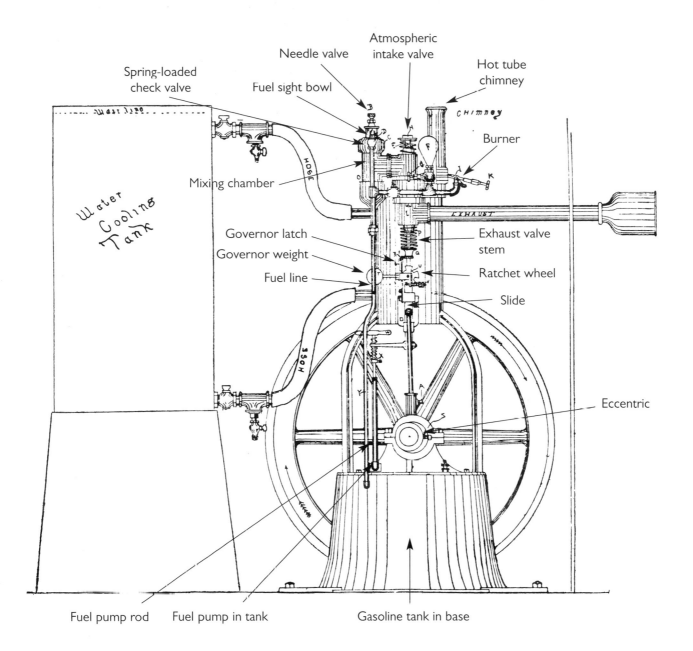

Spring-loaded
check valve

Needle valve

Fuel sight bowl

Atmospheric
intake valve

Hot tube
chimney

Burner

Mixing chamber

Governor latch

Governor weight

Fuel line

Exhaust valve
stem

Ratchet wheel

Slide

Eccentric

Water
Cooling
Tank

Fuel pump rod

Fuel pump in tank

Gasoline tank in base

How the Olds Worked

The Olds is interesting for the manner in which it avoids the use of gears and for its general simplicity. An eccentric on the crankshaft drove a vertical rod that operated a ratchet wheel with four notches and lobes. Each notch and lobe of the ratchet wheel was indexed and timed to the crankshaft's rotation. For example, one low-point on the ratchet corresponded with a closed exhaust valve on the compression stroke. The next time the wheel indexed, it opened the valve for the exhaust stroke. A pendulum-style governor next to the ratchet wheel would, when the engine had reached maximum rpm, push a blade beneath the exhaust valve stem holding it open and allowing the engine to coast until speed was reduced. At that time, the governor was unlatched and normal operation resumed.

The eccentric-driven rod also operated a fuel pump in the tank. Gasoline was pumped up to the top of the engine where it both fed the hot tube burner and entered, through a spring-loaded check valve, a sight bowl to provide fuel for the cylinder. A needle valve atop the sight bowl adjusted the drip of fuel down into a chamber where it mixed with an incoming stream of air, the vapor being drawn into the cylinder through the atmospheric inlet valve. Excess fuel from the mixing chamber returned to the tank.

SAMSON

Owner: Lester Bowman

Condition: Original

Year of Manufacture: Approximately 1902

Place of Manufacture: Stockton, California

Type: Model N, four-cycle with throttling governor

Fuel: Distillate or natural gas

Ignition: Low-tension, make-and-break igniter

Number of Cylinders: 1

Bore x Stroke: 4.75" x 8"

HP @ RPM: 2 1/2 @ 350

Weight: 800 lbs.

Dimensions: 23.5" flywheels, 44" high

Original Application: Ran a Samson centrifugal pump on the Kinnefick ranch in San Joaquin county

Note: the battery box is original. Some 2 1/2 feet long by 18" high and wide, it was designed to accommodate six Edison Type Q batteries. Instead of battery acid, potash mixed with water (and oil to prevent evaporation) was the liquid used in these batteries. The batteries were one-gallon stone jars in which the potash reacted with zinc to develop about 3/4 volts. Today, a modern, 12-volt battery is used.

If ever an engine was the product of its environment, the Samson would be among the first to be named. From the Samson factory in Stockton, California, these engines emerged first in the dozens, then in the hundreds, and ultimately in the thousands, many to serve as pumping engines in the fertile San Joaquin River Delta. It was an application of the most demanding sort.

Consider the record of a three-cylinder, 150-horsepower Samson that drove a 30-inch Samson centrifugal pump mounted on a barge used in land reclamation efforts. During a period of high water of biblical proportions in the winter of 1911, it was reported that this engine was started up on January 28th and ran for 40 days and nights under full power. It had the capacity to pump 35,000 gallons of water per minute and drain the equivalent of six feet of water from an acre per hour. "This is work requiring absolute reliability," said a magazine in 1912, "for there is no time for tinkering and repairs during a flood."

While stationary pumping applications were always a Samson mainstay, marine versions of these robust

engines also found a ready market among tugs and workboats in the California delta, elsewhere on the West Coast, and in export markets as well. Samson even introduced its engine in its own tractor which, with its wide steel "sieve grip" wheels was designed for use on the soft delta soil. Eventually, a Samson truck would also be made. All traded on the suggestion implicit in the company name and possessed, the advertising copy always said, "the strength of Samson in every part."

These engines were the brainchild of a mechanically gifted, straight-talking young man named John Kroyer who started the Samson Iron Works in 1897. Kroyer, then 28 years old, was a Danish immigrant who brought with him to the United States his skills as a machinist. These he promptly augmented by gaining experience as a foundryman with Chicago's Crane Company, then among the country's largest iron manufacturing industries. After 18 months at Crane, Kroyer moved on to foundries in the Pacific Northwest and then to California and the Chico Iron Works, the Holt Company, and the Globe Iron Works. In an era when the metallurgy connected with internal combustion engines was something of an emerging art, John Kroyer learned and refined all the formulas he needed and he relied on no outside suppliers for key engine castings.

It is clear that, before he started his own company, John Kroyer had a concise vision of where he was headed. He recognized the great market potential right in his part of California for a high-efficiency, engine-driven water pump. He created just such a pump and then the engine to drive it. Kroyer had gained internal combustion engine experience with previous employers. Apparently, he had his own prototype in operation in 1897 although he recognized that it was not a design suitable for volume production. The best guess now is

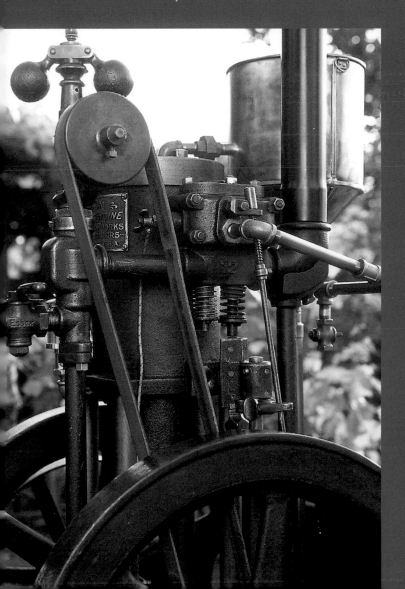

that the first Samson engine built for sale was constructed in 1898. On July 9, 1902, the company was incorporated as the Samson Iron Works. With incorporation came a new, two-story factory that was enlarged in December, 1906, and at least twice thereafter. By 1908, the company was reported to be building 1,000 engines annually.

The engine shown here is from the early days of Samson production and is among the earliest known engines with a distillate vaporizer. This emphasis on distillate as a fuel was a special interest of Kroyer's. At the time, "California Grade #1 Distillate" cost about half the price of gasoline, and Kroyer experimented with ways of adapting his engine to run on the fuel. His first efforts included a complex and ungainly fuel tank pre-heater device but he eventually developed a successful vaporizer that permitted the engine to be switched to distillate after starting and warming up on gasoline. Only the 2 1/2-horsepower model was a vertical. The others were horizontals.

In 1918, John Kroyer sold his company to William C. Durant, creator of General Motors, for $400,000. It proved a better deal for Kroyer than for GM, which liquidated Samson several years later, having found no commercial success with the tractors, which were Durant's chief reason for buying the company in the first place. As for John Kroyer, he died at age 76 on September 14, 1945. His was, all in all, a great success story, and John Kroyer could have been a sort of poster boy for the American immigrant who made good in California's central valley, a place as fertile for the marketing of durable, hard-working, internal combustion engines as it was for growing crops.

Governor

Stationary electrode

Copper cooling water tank

Valve chest (or pre-combustion chamber)

Water inlet pipe

Exhaust valve

Atmospheric intake valve

Igniter rod

Inlet for natural gas hook-up

Vertical shaft driven off the crankshaft operates the igniter rod and the exhaust valve.

How the Samson Model N Worked

On the intake stroke, vacuum draws liquid distillate fuel past a needle through the atmospheric inlet valve into the pre-chamber or valve chest. The resulting vapor is mixed with air to create the explosive charge. A vertical side shaft with a face cam, driven by the crankshaft, operates both the igniter rod and the exhaust valve. The make-and-break igniter is powered by four Edison potash batteries, which supply current to the low-tension coil. Both coil and batteries are housed in the Samson battery box.

Big Power for a New Century

NEW ERA

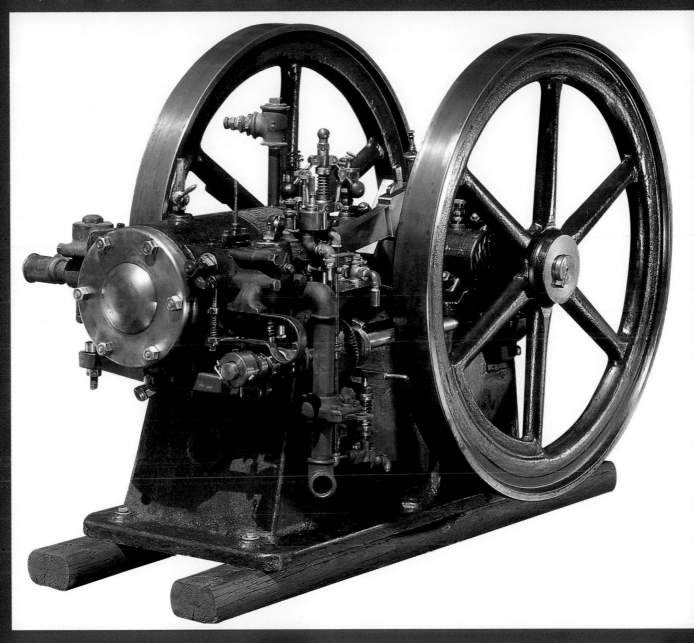

Owner: John Rex

Manufacturer: New Era Iron Works

Year of Manufacture: Circa 1903

Place of Manufacture: Dayton, Ohio

Type: 4-cycle

Fuel: Liquid or gas (can be changed from one to the other while running)

Ignition: Low-tension with make-and-break igniter

Number of Cylinders: 1

Bore x Stroke: 7" x 10"

HP @ RPM: 5 @ 240

Weight: 2,300 lbs.

Dimensions: 40" flywheels; floor space 40" wide x 60" long

Original Application: Power for woodshop in Wilmington, Vermont

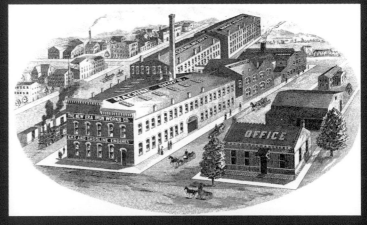

In September of 1896, the owner of a factory in Allegheny City, Pennsylvania, sat down to write a letter to the maker whose gas engine he had recently purchased. Like many who went engine shopping in that period, Mr. A. F. Schwerd made a careful study of the machines available to him and, in fact, took a full year in making up his mind. He decided upon an engine named, its maker believed, for the wholly new world that would be built on the strength of internal combustion. This engine was the "New Era." The company and its products were the brainchild of James R. Johnston who, it turned out, was not alone in selecting "New Era" as a moniker. At least four automobile manufacturers called themselves "New Era" in the period 1901 – 1933.

Mr. Schwerd's engine selection proved to be more fortunate than some because he reported that "I finally closed in on a New Era Engine, and in a few words can honestly say that I believe from what I can learn that it's the only engine in and around Pittsburgh that has given practically no trouble in operating."

The engine in question was a 60-horsepower model that was employed driving machinery on the three

floors of Mr. Schwerd's factory for 80 cents to a dollar per 10-hour day. Mr. Schwerd's letter was one of several that New Era published as testimonials, a common effort by engine builders to demonstrate the great satisfaction that their products were delivering. At the time this particular testimonial

Fuel admission pick-up blade

was written, the proprietors at New Era were doing their best to establish themselves as makers of a quality product during what was, in fact, still the pioneer period of the industry. Not only was New Era facing competition from other companies in the Midwest and the East, but right there in Ohio, where, in Springfield, the Springfield Gas Engine Company and the Foos Gas Engine Company were beginning to exercise what would prove to be considerable muscle of their own.

Quite early in the history of the New Era Iron Works Company, it was decided to focus on large engines. Although Mr. Johnston once proclaimed himself confident that he could build a single-cylinder engine of 500 horsepower, the most powerful New Era seems to have been 125 horsepower, which could well have been, as the company claimed, "the largest single cylinder Gas Engine built in the United States." News of the sale of these big engines occurred with some regularity. In 1898 alone, a 100-horsepower New Era went to a shoe manufacturer in Lancaster, Ohio, and an 80 hp model was sold to a phosphate manufacturer in Columbus, to cite just two examples. Overall, the model range extended from 5- to 125-horsepower engines.

Although the cylinder head region of the New Era appears complex, the company stressed the absence of rods, elbows, arms and eccentrics found on many other designs, components liable to wear and then require expert adjustment. New Era, by contrast, used a single side shaft driven by spiral gears. Cams on the forward end of the shaft drove the make-and-break igniter, exhaust valve, intake valve, and the fuel admission valve. The igniter cam is a spiral-type with a slow rise and an instantaneous drop to produce the rapid opening of the igniter points. The camshaft was also fitted with a gear that operated the vertical governor which, at the appointed speed, slid the cam follower away from the fuel admission stem and prevented fuel entry.

The exhaust valve rocker included a roller cam follower, typical of the engine's mechanical elegance. The New Era featured an unusual auxiliary exhaust port cast into the cylinder. This port was uncovered by the piston at the end of its downstroke and contributed significantly to the prompt evacuation of exhaust gas so that the exhaust valve itself was subjected to less heat and thus had an increased life expectancy.

The entirely original engine shown here is the smallest of New Era's offerings but possesses the same architecture as the larger engines. New Era purchasers had a choice of two connecting rods styles. One was the "marine rod," a round rod forged at each end with bolted brass-bearing journal boxes. The other was the "strap style" familiar to steam engine men. Flat, made

of forged iron, the phosphor bronze journal boxes were held in place by a gib and key. This latter rod is found on this engine. With its chunky, nearly square proportions, remnants of gold pinstriping, and many, obviously high quality machined parts, this New Era is an impressive survivor of early 20th century internal combustion.

Starting the New Era

The first step is to see that the cylinder water jacket is full and then to oil all the moving parts and adjust the lubricators. Once these tasks have been accomplished, the spark lever is moved to retard the spark, the compression release atop the cylinder is opened and the battery is connected. Next, the air shutter on the air inlet pipe is opened a third of the way and the gas cock also opened a third of a turn. Then the flywheels are turned until one or more explosions occur. At the point, the compression release is closed and the engine will pick up speed. The spark can be advanced and the gas cock and air shutter adjusted for the smoothest running.

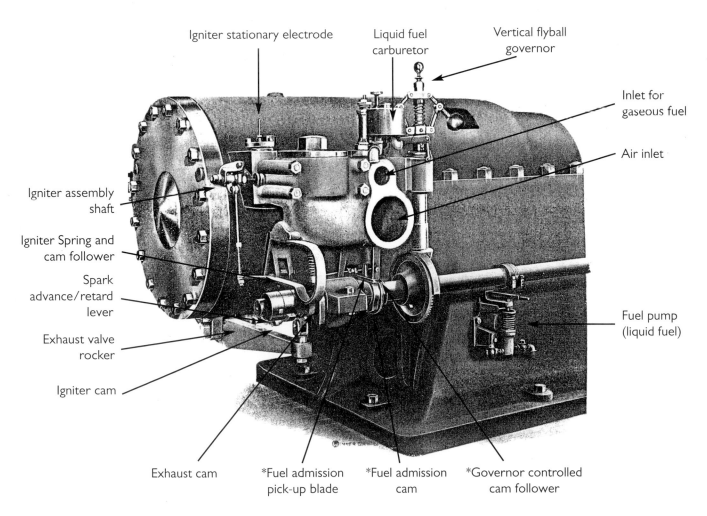

Igniter stationary electrode

Liquid fuel carburetor

Vertical flyball governor

Inlet for gaseous fuel

Air inlet

Igniter assembly shaft

Igniter Spring and cam follower

Spark advance/retard lever

Exhaust valve rocker

Igniter cam

Fuel pump (liquid fuel)

Exhaust cam

*Fuel admission pick-up blade

*Fuel admission cam

*Governor controlled cam follower

* The engine's hit and miss operation – its speed limited by cutting off fuel flow – is controlled by these components

The Industrialist's Vision
FAIRBANKS

Fairbanks-Morse Type T

Owner: Harry J. Garman
Manufacturer: Fairbanks-Morse
Year of Manufacture: Circa 1912
Place of Manufacture: Beloit, Wisconsin
Type: 4-cycle
Fuel: Gasoline/Kerosene
Ignition: Make-and-break
Number of Cylinders: 1
Bore x Stroke: 8 1/2" x 15"
HP @ RPM: 4 @ 400
Weight: 1,550 lbs.
Dimensions: 41" flywheels, Overall height 56 1/2"
Original Application: Powered generator for
electrical light and power

Those within the great enterprise that was Fairbanks-Morse generally referred to the company's founder as the "controlling genius" behind the whole operation. This man was Charles Hosmer Morse. Born in 1833 in St. Johnsbury, Vermont, Morse grew up in a pre-industrial New England of small villages, towns, and farms. It was a world dominated by horse-drawn plows and power generated by fast-flowing water that worked the mills and, as time wore on, by steam. Morse did much to change that world. He did this not as an inventor but as a businessman who combined a perceptive vision of the impact that internal combustion engines could have with significant managerial and organizational skills.

The multi-faceted corporation that would grow from Morse's efforts was based initially on an invention of two brothers in St. Johnsbury named Erasmus and Thaddeus Fairbanks. In 1830, the brothers who were then manufacturing cast iron plows and stoves patented what soon became known as the platform scale. There were lots of plow and stove makers, but nobody else had a scale like that of the Fairbanks brothers. In 1850 when he was 17 years old, Charles Morse went to work for the E & T Fairbanks Company. Seven years later, he moved to Chicago where the "western" sales branch operated as Fairbanks Greenleaf & Company.

These were good years for the company and Charles Morse developed significant skills in sales and, as it turned out, in sizing up the potential market for a new product. Business was prospering for Greenleaf & Fairbanks when, on an October night in 1871, a fire began in Chicago that would ultimately destroy some 18,000 buildings. The fire marked the end of Mr. Greenleaf's role in the company for, after that, the business was known as Fairbanks, Morse & Company. Now, Morse began adding product lines that would make the company a kind of early conglomerate. In 1880, Morse took an interest in the Eclipse Windmill Company in Beloit, Wisconsin, beginning a great expansion of that business as the Eclipse Wind Engine Company. A steam engine builder, the Williams Engine Works was acquired in about 1889. Then, in 1893, Morse acquired the rights to an internal combustion engine developed by James Charter. It proved to be a good business decision for Morse, especially since the same farmers who had bought Eclipse wind

Charles Hosmer Morse (1833–1921). (Courtesy of the Charles Hosmer Morse Museum of American Art)

mills were an obvious market for the engines. The Fairbanks-Charter name soon gave way to the label that would become known throughout the world as Fairbanks-Morse.

The engines pictured here are merely two of the dozens of models produced by the company. Oldtimers within the company stated that the "N" derivation referred to naptha and that the N became the company's first commercially successful gasoline engine. The Type T derived from the R, the company's first vertical model introduced in 1895. The T was often called the "electrical engine." Equipped with wide, heavy flywheels to drive a wide belt connected to a generator, the goal was produce an engine that would drive the generator at a steady 400 rpm and provide flicker-free lighting. Its enclosed base made for clean operation. Engines like this were developed to bring the miracle of electricity to rural homes throughout America.

Exhaust pipe

Automatic inlet valve

Water exit

Drip oiler for bearings and cylinder

Inlet for water

Fairbanks-Morse Type T

Make-and-break igniter

Carburetor

Water pump

Water drain

Needle valve

FAIRBANKS, MORSE & CO.
TYPE T

Fuel return

Gas line

Exhaust pushrod

Exhaust cam drive gear

Magneto

Magneto drive gear

Lubricators for camshaft

Fuel pump

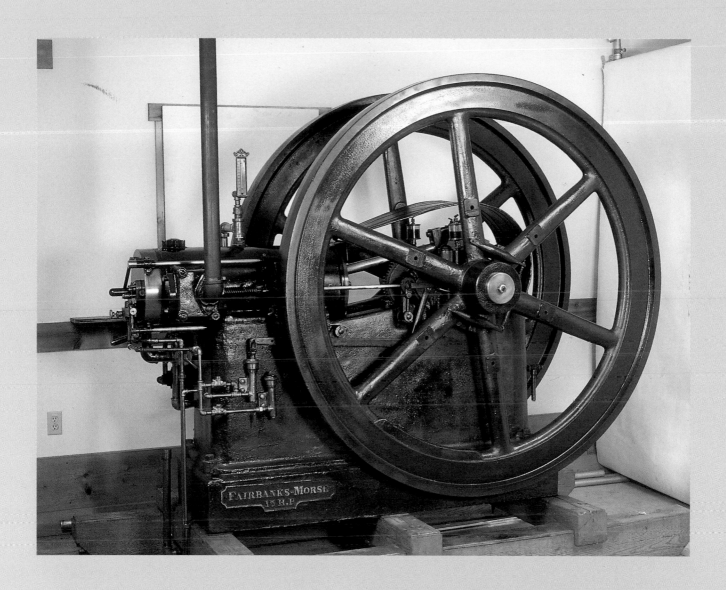

Fairbanks-Morse Model N

Owner: Mary Ellen Susong
Manufacturer: Fairbanks-Morse
Year of Manufacture: 1905
Place of Manufacture: Beloit, Wisconsin
Type: 4-cycle
Fuel: Gasoline
Ignition: Make-and-break
Number of Cylinders: 1
Bore x Stroke: 8 1/2" x 15"
HP: 15
Weight: Approx. 8,000 lbs.
Original Application: Used to charge batteries for
   New England Bell

Owner: H. J. Garman
Year of Manufacture: Circa 1905
Place of Manufacture: Mystic, Connecticut
Type: Two-cycle
Fuel: Gasoline
Ignition: Low-tension make-and-break
Number of Cylinders: 1
Bore x Stroke: 5 1/2" x 5"
HP @ RPM: 6 @ 500
Dimensions: 17" flywheel, 30" high x 26" long
Weight:
Original Application: Power for workboat

James W. Lathrop was a needle peddler from Worcester, Massachusetts, who made a small fortune building marine engines in Mystic, Connecticut. In April, 1924, when he sat down to tell the world about his company in a retrospective for *Motor Boat* magazine, Lathrop proved himself a rather taciturn Yankee who preferred to let his product speak for itself. He had little to say but did share that he had just received an order from a fisherman who had bought a Lathrop 24 years earlier. Now, the fisherman was building a new boat and wanted a new Lathrop to power it. It was James Lathrop's idea of the best sort of advertising.

Like numerous others, Lathrop was influenced to some degree by the earliest of the East Coast marine engine builders, Palmer. It was a problem with a Palmer's igniter in a friend's boat that prompted what became the Lathrop Motor Company. The engine produced was simple and straightforward, a two-port, two-cycle. This was the same approach taken by Palmer and Mianus and was distinct from that other successful Connecticut maker, Bridgeport. The latter built a three-port engine with somewhat higher rpm potential and greater speed control.

The two-port engines, with their heavy flywheels, were well accepted by fishermen who found the moderate rpm and excellent slow- or high-speed perfor-

mance met all their needs. The Lathrop's castings were heavy and well finished and its igniter mechanism of generous proportions. It was an engine that might last forever; especially in fresh water and that may have been where the engine presented here spent its working life. Its water jackets, usually the prime destroyer of marine engines that operated in salt water unless the jackets were thoroughly flushed, are open and solid. Overall, this is as nice a Lathrop as one is likely to find and an engine that commercial fishermen by the thousands depended upon for their lives and livelihood.

The Titan from Chicago

INTERNATIONAL HARVESTER

Hot tube fuel tank

Water tank

Brake lever

Hot tube chimney

Seat

Igniter

Exhaust

Battery box

Exhaust valve rocker

Fuel tank (in base)

Ignition Dynamo

Owner: Clyde Burkholder
Manufacturer: International Harvester
Corporation
Year of Manufacture: 1905
Place of Manufacture: Milwaukee, Wisconsin
Type: 4-cycle
Fuel: Gasoline
Ignition: Make-and-break igniter/Hot tube
Number of Cylinders: 1
Bore x Stroke: 7 1/2" x 12"
HP: 12
Dimensions: 4 1/2' flywheel
Weight: 2,300 lbs.
Original Application: Unknown

In 1902, two great agricultural equipment manufacturers joined with several smaller companies
in a merger engineered by J. P. Morgan &
Company. The two were the Deering Harvester
Company and the McCormick Harvesting Machine
Company, which traced its ancestry to the mechanical
reaper perfected by Cyrus McCormick. One impetus
for this coming together was to pool resources to cover
the expense of tooling up for production of stationary
engines for farm use on a major scale. The first engines
were built between late 1903 and June 1904 at the
Deering Works in Chicago. For the 1905 season, some
3,000 horizontal engines like the one shown here were
built at the new Corporation's Milwaukee works.

Now, International Harvester was poised for what
would become an enormous and varied industrial output. In 1907, the company introduced a motorized
"autobuggy," large gas engines for municipal and factory power and, as the years wore on, ever more
engines, automobiles, and trucks. Just how mighty this
conglomerate was can be indicated by the scope of the
exhibits it presented at the nation's major agricultural
expositions. At San Diego in 1915, IHC presented
some 150 machines of various sorts and a giant model
of a farm shown with different activities to match each
of the four seasons. There was row after row of tractors
and engines, the latter operating on compressed air at
slow rpm so visitors could readily examine the
mechanics of their operation. Outside the exhibit hall,
the company had a five-acre demonstration field and
had actually planted a citrus orchard in which its tractors could be seen at work. An irrigation plant was
equipped with engines to pump water, and there was a
motorized baler to bale hay.

The engine shown here is among International's
earliest. Not only is it complete in all respects, but it
blends the primitive with the sophisticated to result in
a most intriguing machine. The more sophisticated
aspects of the engine include its ignition system. It has

both a make-and-break system and a hot tube. Batteries
housed in a box beneath the driver's seat supplied the
current needed for starting. The "autosparker," which
was driven off one of the flywheels, generated electricity for ignition once the engine was running. A
copper, gravity-feed tank supplied the hot tube which,
according to the engine's owner, appears never to have
been used. A more primitive, yet ingenious, compo-
nent is the cooling system. There is no water pump.
Instead, as the engine warms up, its heat siphons water
from the bottom of the tank into the water jacket. The
water then flows out of the top of the jacket and back
to the tank.

Portable engines like this had begun to become
important factors on American farms soon after 1900
when the farmer realized, as *The Gas Engine* magazine
reported in January, 1904, that "combustion engines do
work that has heretofore cost him $20 a month, the
board of a farm hand. Builders of this type of engine
can show hundreds and thousands of inquiries to prove
that this demand is only in its infancy. The little
engine on the farm does wonders."

"Not Like Others"

WESTERN

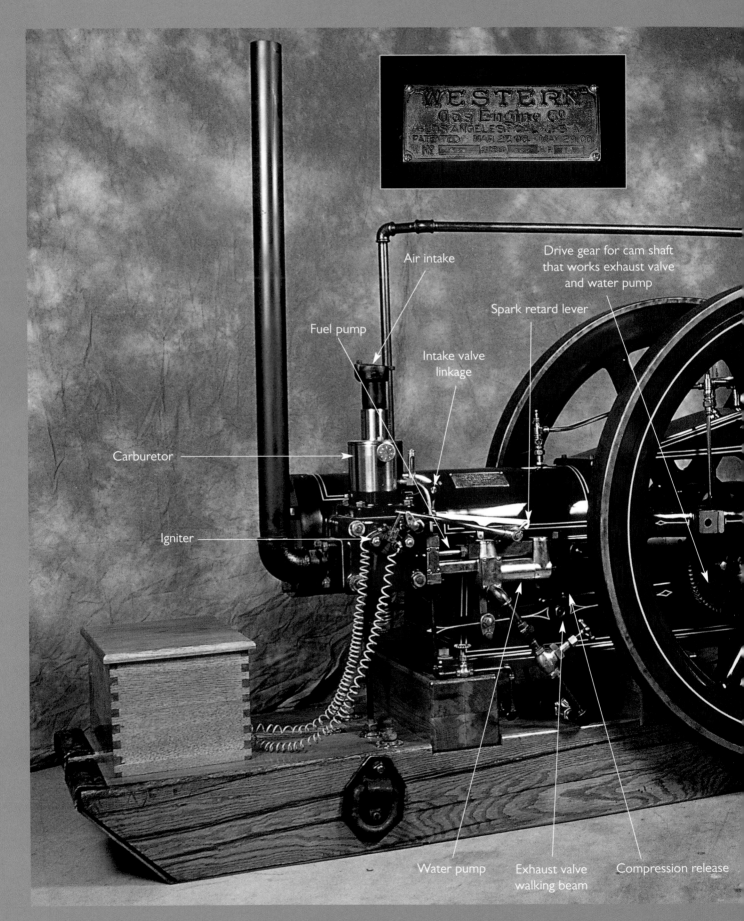

Air intake

Drive gear for cam shaft
that works exhaust valve
and water pump

Spark retard lever

Fuel pump

Intake valve
linkage

Carburetor

Igniter

Water pump

Exhaust valve
walking beam

Compression release

In January, 1915, a great fair opened in San Diego, California, that presented, among other things, all that was most modern in the world of internal combustion engines and machinery. Here, in buildings with names like the "Palace of Machinery," the "Tractor Building," and "Machinery Hall," exhibitors from around the country came to display their wares in often quite sophisticated exhibits. In the Palace of Agriculture, the Holt Tractor Company actually constructed an English-style cottage surrounded by a brick wall that enclosed its entire model line-up. Over in Machinery Hall, one A. R. Johnston was busily answering questions of those looking at the engines built by the Western Gas Engine Company. He reported to the press the receipt "of quite a number of orders for mining and irrigation purposes as well as for the operation of dredges for Alaska."

Although the West Coast engine industry was dominated by San Francisco-area companies, Western carved out a niche for itself from its base in Los Angeles. What had begun as the Western Iron Works in 1887 evolved into the Western Gas Engine Company in 1905. By then, the company had been building engines for about five years. The first Western was a quite unusual four-cycle, gearless "reversible" model — the "1900" for the year of its introduction — that could run forward or backward. This capability certainly would have been advantageous in the oil field, which was among several markets that Western pursued. The engine's other main selling point was the ability to run on a variety of fuels including gas, gasoline, distillate, or crude oil.

Owner: Robert Critz
Manufacturer: Western Engine Company
Year of Manufacture: January 15, 1907
Place of Manufacture: Los Angeles, California
Type: 4-cycle
Fuel: Distillate
Ignition: Low-tension make-and-break
Number of Cylinders: 1
Bore x Stroke: 8 1/4" x 16"
HP @ RPM: 25 @ 280
Weight: 3,500 lbs.
Dimensions: 54" flywheel, approximate floor
    space: 4 1/2' x 7'
Original Application: Operated a mine hoist.

Starting the Western

Prior to starting, the carburetor must be filled with fuel. (There is no provision for using the fuel pump to do this as the pump would somehow have to be disconnected from the gear-driven camshaft.) With the carburetor filled, the compression release, mounted on the walking beam near its pivot point, is opened. The spark is retarded using a small lever above the fuel pump. The engine is now ready to start.

Close-up of the igniter. The arm that drives the moveable electrode is operated by the same rod that works the water pump and fuel pump (see overall portrait). The rod itself is operated by a short camshaft that is gear driven off the crankshaft.

The Western's big lubricator, mounted on the crank guard, directs oil to all the needed areas. A filling with 30 weight oil generally suffices for a day's operation.

This all sounded better than it actually was, for the first Western developed a reputation for cranky starting, and may have possessed some significant mechanical flaws. In the summer of 1904, a new model was introduced. This was a non-reversible engine with a gear-driven valve mechanism and hit-or-miss, centrifugal governor that latched the exhaust valve open. Perhaps its most unusual feature is an eccentric arm that operates the water pump, fuel pump, igniter, and intake valve! This eccentric is on the same shaft to which the timing gear is affixed. A cam lobe works the long, horizontal exhaust valve rocker arm. Both valves are positioned vertically, unlike the earlier model's, and are much less subject to wearing out of the valve stems. A patented vaporizer could handle gasoline but was also, said Western, " designed especially for California No. 2 Distillate and Denatured Alcohol, handling these as well or better than Eastern-built engines handle gasoline."

By 1906, Western claimed to be the largest exclusive builder of stationary engines on the Pacific Coast. "Not Like Others" is how the company positioned its new engine in its ads. The beautiful engine shown here — the result of a nine-month restoration — is the new model "1905" Western. Because the company kept a file card on every engine it made, and because many of those cards have survived, this machine is known to have been built on January 15, 1907. Like so many other Westerns, this engine was used to power a mine hoist. It was delivered to the Skylark Mining Company in Goldfield, Nevada, where it was used until 1916 when a California Mining Company bought it. In 1921, it was sold to the Pacific Borax Company in Death Valley.

Although Western was successfully selling its clever engines to mining companies, farmers, ranchers, oil and gas drillers, and municipal water works, markets that were out of its reach including those for marine and diesel engines. The solution to this challenge lay up in San Francisco with a company that had been founded in 1886, a year before Western. This was the Enterprise Engine and Foundry Company. From 1886 until 1916, Enterprise had been a major supplier of castings for Bay Area engine companies. In 1917, it built its own gasoline/distillate engine and, two years later, a diesel. Then, in 1921, Enterprise obtained rights to the Vickers common rail fuel injection system and this,

together with efforts at improving power-to-weight ratios, resulted in a quite successful engine business.

Western enthusiast Terry Hathaway, who has extensively researched the company, believes that Western may have bought or assembled and rebadged Enterprise engines in the period leading up to 1923. In 1924, however, the two companies merged, and the resultant engines, both stationary and marine, were generally known by the Western-Enterprise label. The new company also developed an airplane engine in 1925 only to drop the effort two years later to focus on the core business. One result was a 500 horsepower engine with a 15" bore and 21" stroke. According to one of Enterprise's long-time executives, the larger horsepower engines were built in San Francisco and the smaller models in Los Angeles.

Although Western introduced a variety of new products during the 1930s, increased competition and, perhaps, a lack of managerial foresight resulted in the company's closing in 1938. Enterprise, however, continued, suggesting that the nature of the merger was not one that had totally comingled the financial operation of the two companies. Beginning in 1933, Enterprise introduced a new line of lighter weight, higher-speed diesels using Bosch or Bendix fuel injection equipment. The company survived World War II and in 1948, Enterprise — still doing business under its original name — published a full-page ad showing its latest, enclosed diesel engine that had been recently purchased by the town of Carlin, Nevada, to drive its new power plant.

This two-cylinder Enterprise marine engine was probably built in 1917 or 1918. The Enterprise Foundry Company was located in San Francisco at 19th Street.

"To build the best gas engine we know how"

UNION

Essex oilers with wooden knobs

Throttle body (atmospheric inlet valve behind throttle body)

Throttle linkage

Gear-driven, throttling governor

Needle valve

Carburetor with screw-top lid and float

Preheater manifold

Owner: Anton Affentranger
Manufacturer: Union Gas Engine Company
Year of Manufacture: October 29, 1909 (Serial #6071)
Place of Manufacture: San Francisco
Type: 4-cycle
Fuel: Gasoline
Ignition: Low-tension make-and-break
Number of Cylinders: 1
Bore x Stroke: 5" x 6"
HP @ RPM: 4 @ 400 (Union tests demonstrated an actual 4.6 hp)
Weight: 1,185 pounds (Shipping weight)
Dimensions: 28" flywheels; 43 1/2" high
Original Application: Pump house

The ultimate result of the patent suits between the Regan Vapor Engine Company and the Pacific Gas Engine Company was the formation of a new firm that would be among the most long-lived of all the California engine builders. The Union Gas Engine Company was formed in May 1892. John F. Daley, who had been secretary of Pacific, became the first president. Mora Barrett, who had been listed as Pacific's manager and in whose name several patents were awarded, became secretary treasurer. Others were involved as well and the company was well capitalized with $300,000. Union's 1894 brochure stated that the engine was "the outcome of the consolidation of the Regan and the Pacific Companies' patents and embodies the joint results of the two companies' previous experience as manufacturers of this class of motor."

Union immediately embarked on an ambitious program of development that included a patented vaporizer that replaced the old "carburetor." Among the latter's demerits was the fact that the air that passed over the gasoline absorbed only the lighter more volatile part while allowing the heavier portion to remain and form a residue. Improved igniters were developed and the company always stressed the advantage of electric ignition over hot tube. New vertical and horizontal models were introduced, fuelling such rapid growth that Union could, by 1894, claim nearly 2000 sales on the Pacific Coast alone. Union's assertion that year that it had "manufactured more Gasoline Engines than any other company in America" could well have been accurate.

Among the men most responsible for the advances at Union was the Scottish-born chief engineer, William Corson, whose worked touched every aspect of the engines. Several years after Union's founding, Corson would replace Barrett as Union's secretary-treasurer and William J. Casey replaced Daley as president. By then, there was simply no stopping Union. Its

robust sideshaft horizontal engines became fixtures in mines, pump houses, and power stations, and its marine engines were widely sold on the coast and in export markets. Together with engineer and company vice president Stanley Page, Corson designed a Union airplane engine. According to Charles Winslow, engineer and historian of the West Coast engine industry, a Union was the first aviation engine to pass a Navy 48-hour test. Eventually, Union would turn to diesel engines and in 1930, it changed its name to the Union Diesel Engine Company. Sales of parts for these engines were not discontinued until 1996.

The pleasingly proportioned Union engine shown here is in entirely original condition. Surviving documents reveal that a Union mechanic whose name was Thayer erected it. Such engines, with their magical patina of old paint highlighted by different color metals, hark back to the early days of internal combustion engine production. It was a time when Union could stress the convenience of interchangeable parts, an idea that had posed a significant challenge only a few years before. Union guaranteed its engines for one year but many provided reliable services for decades. The engine's current owner reports that he had the old Union running the day after he brought it home and that it still operates reliably some 90 years after it left Union's San Francisco factory.

A Classic of Endurance and Power

NIAGARA

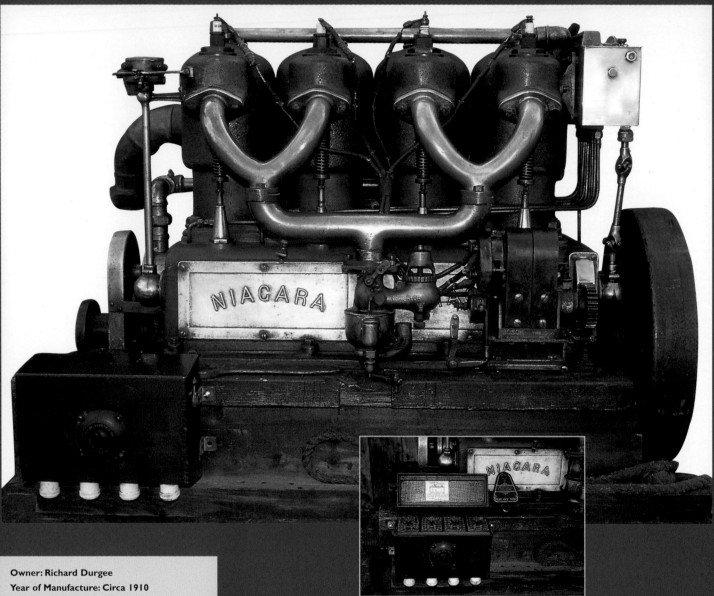

Owner: Richard Durgee

Year of Manufacture: Circa 1910

Place of Manufacture: Buffalo, New York

Type: 4-cycle

Fuel: Gasoline

Ignition: Bosch magneto and battery

Number of Cylinders: 4

Bore x Stroke: 3 1/2" x 4 1/2"

HP @ RPM: 15 @ 600 – 900

Weight: 525 pounds

Dimensions: 44" long x 32" high, 18" flywheel

Original Application: Engine for displacement launch

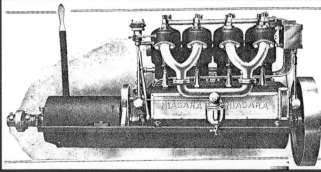

NIAGARA
THE MOTOR OF QUALITY

4-cycle in 2, 4, and 6 cylinders, 5 to 90 h.p., with short or long base, according to requirements, for **Cruising, Racing, Fishing, Freighting.**
Every NIAGARA is fitted with mechanical force feed oiler, rotary or plunger pump and high tension dual magneto, if desired. NIAGARA crankshafts are hammer-forged out of 35 point carbon steel and have two bearings to every throw. The NIAGARA is recognized throughout the world as **Powerful, Dependable, Economical, Graceful.**
It has no intricate, complicated or superfluous parts. Just motor, that's all.
Investigate. Better be sure than sorry.
Send for catalog and Book of Evidence.

NIAGARA GASOLINE MOTOR CO.
192-202 Breckenridge St. Buffalo, N. Y., U. S. A.

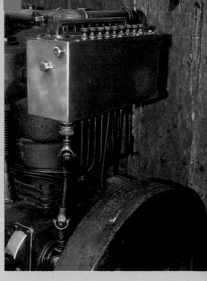

Some measure of the demand for marine engines in America can be judged by the fact that in the city of Buffalo, New York, alone, four significant companies were begun at about the same time and each remained in business for a meaningful period of time. These companies included Buffalo, Peerless, Sterling, and Niagara. What ultimately became known as the Niagara Motors Corporation was known originally as the Ducro Manufacturing Company. It was founded in 1904 by Louis M. Ducro and, from its earliest days, the Niagara engines it produced were recognized for straightforward design, and high quality. Possessing large displacement and heavy-duty components, the Niagaras were well-suited to powering the displacement-type hulls so typical of the period.

Ducro's engines received a big boost in 1909 when a wealthy Buffalo motorboat racer named Ralph Sidway chose a Niagara to power his *Arab III* to a race win on the Niagara River. Although Sidway selected Sterling engines for subsequent Arabs, Niagara went on to make a name for itself during the next several years, winning numerous trophies both in the U.S. and abroad. It was probably some time during the 1910 – 1912 period that Ducro sold the company to Charles Narraway whose name would be the one most closely associated with Niagara from that time on. The name was changed to Niagara Gasoline Motor Company and, after World War I, to Niagara Motors Corporation.

By 1912, demand for Niagara's rather extensive lineup was large enough to prompt the purchase of a 2 1/2 acre property in Dunkirk, New York, where a new factory was built. Here, engine production continued into the 1930s and, after that time, connecting rods were made. This factory was still standing, although closed down, in the early 1970s when a local boat enthusiast discovered it, full of parts, engines and even the line-shafts that drove the machinery. Among other things discovered by Lou Deering were records of each engine sold by Niagara dating back to the company's beginnings, about 3000 in all.

The Niagara pictured here is a genuine "artifact," one of the pitifully few marine engines that have come down to us in completely intact and original condition. It is a classic of the period, a T-head engine with twin ignition, an engine representative of a whole generation of pre-World War I marine and automotive powerplants. The Niagara's survival was due in part to the fact that it was a fresh-water engine. It was originally installed in a launch used in the Thousand Islands region of New York. After it was taken out of service in World War II, the old Niagara was purchased by an antique shop owner in Chippewa Bay. From there, it went to a boatbuilder who kept it in an attic for about a decade until it was purchased by Long Island marine engine collector and restorer Danny Acierno. Eventually, it came into the possession of its current owner.

This Niagara is a presence. It speaks to us of a quite different epoch, an age of brass and bronze and cast iron. A bundle of tubing makes its way from the force-feed oiler to key points on the machine. The ubiquitous Schebler updraft carburetor is all there. So is the original coil box and timer. Bronze pins hold the cam lobes to the camshafts, one on either side, of course. One doesn't see an engine like the Niagara everyday. And that is why it is included here, a surviving treasure evocative of how people went powerboating during the first decade of the 20th century.

FOOS

Governor drive gears

Magneto

Priming cup (nut unscrews for inspection)

Intake chamber

Exhaust pipe

Exhaust valave rocker arm

Stationary electrode

Intake valve rocker arm

Moveable electrode

Air intake pipe

THE FOOS
GAS ENGINE CO.
SPRINGFIELD, O.
PATENTED
No 23722   SPEED 200   H.P. 40

Owner: Nathan Lillibridge
Manufacturer: Foos Gas Engine Works
Year of Manufacture: Circa 1910
Place of Manufacture: Springfield, Ohio
Type: 4-cycle
Fuel: Gasoline, kerosene, illuminating gas
Ignition: Wipe spark, high tension magneto
Number of Cylinders: 1
Bore x Stroke: 12 1/2" x 20"
HP @ RPM: 40 @ 300
Weight: 10,000 lbs.
Dimensions: 80" flywheel
Original Application: Drove a water pump in a
   municipal power plant

Among the many curious aspects of internal combustion development in America is the role played by Ohioans. The state was home to a seemingly inordinate number of important industry figures. Among them were Edmund Wilson Roberts, the prolific designer and writer from Sandusky; the Scottish immigrant and diesel innovator in Cleveland, Alexander Winton; the great General Motors scientist and engineer from Loudonville, Charles Kettering; and the pioneering inventor Clark Sintz. Sintz, born in Springfield, was one of several men who made the city a center for engine manufacture, but it was his one-time partner, John Foos, who established the most successful of Springfield's engine companies.

Foos himself was not an inventor. He was, however, a skilled and wealthy businessman who allied himself with the necessary engineering talent. Among the latter was shop foreman Charles Endter who developed the company's signature wipe-spark ignitor. He described it thusly: "The flexible electrode is engaged by the rotary electrode at each rotation by a wiping contact which bends the said flexible electrode till it suddenly snaps off from the rotary electrode with an instantaneous spring action and produces the ignition spark."

The basic architecture of the horizontal Foos engine was developed in 1894 by Harry Voll who had previously worked with Clark Sintz and also had been superintendent of the St. John Sewing Machine Company in Springfield. Among the features of Voll's design was the location of the intake and exhaust valves in easily accessed chests on each side of the cylinder head. The

As beautiful a piece of engine art as one is likely to see anywhere, the Foos is elegant in all details. The detail above shows the drive gears and the governor. The close-up portrait (below) shows the intake chamber. The stationary electrode of the wipe spark igniter protrudes. The moveable electrode is driven by the polished crank. Atop the intake chamber is the priming cup mounted atop a removable fitting that gives access both to the igniter and the intake valve.

gear-driven governor was the work of another Foos foreman named Andrew Sonander, who patented the design in January, 1902. Especially noteworthy were the counterbalance discs mounted on either side of the connecting rod. Forged from steel billets, these discs made for such exceptionally smooth running that Foos catalogs showed the engine operating at its maximum 310 rpm and sitting atop polished steel rollers but not moving.

When the Foos Gas Engine Company was incorporated in 1897, John Foos, was president and his son George was secretary. Then, in 1899, the company was reorganized and John Foos whose business interests (to name a few) had included machinery and implement manufacture, and large investments in the Louisiana sugar industry, stepped aside. His son-in-law Scipio Baker, who had been named president a year earlier, guided the company until he died in 1921. With $150,000 in capital, and a well-conceived, constructed, and finished engine as its core product, Foos was well-positioned to expand, which it did for almost three decades. The company became a centerpiece industry in Springfield which, in addition to manufacturing, also claimed in 1916 to produce more roses than any city in the world. The beautiful Foos shown here is the result of a total restoration that included repairing the engine's cracked frame.

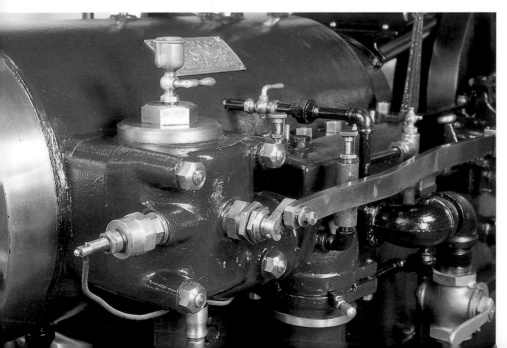

WITTE

Owner: Bill Hazzard
Year of Manufacture: 1911
Place of Manufacture: Kansas City, Missouri
Type: 4-cycle
Fuel: Gasoline
Ignition: Make and Break
Number of Cylinders: 1
Bore x Stroke: 9" x 14"
HP @ RPM: 15 @ 260
Weight: 4,000 lbs.
Dimensions: 52" flywheels
Original Application: Pumping water on an
   estate in Portsmouth, Rhode Island

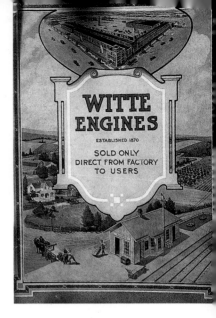

As successful an engine-building entrepreneur as existed during the internal combustion century, Edward H. Witte came from that generation of practical engineers and businessmen who learned a trade from the ground up. Hardworking, self-confident, a journeyman in seven trades by the time was 18 years old, Witte embodied a combination of integrity, business acumen, and mechanical genius of a peculiarly American kind. The robust business that he built was begun and remained in that great city of the nation's center, Kansas City, Missouri. There, he was known as the Henry Ford of the gas engine business and the men who worked in the plant of the Witte Iron Works compared him to the inventive Thomas Edison.

When he looked back on his career in a 1933 interview with the Kansas City Star, Witte, who was then 65 years old, noted that he left school after the fourth grade to begin his apprenticeship with his father. August Witte had been superintendent of the Cincinnati Brass Manufacturing Company (later famous as Lunkenheimer) before he moved to Kansas City and opened the Witte Machine Works in 1870 when Edward was two years old. Under the guidance of his father, Edward Witte became a machinist, brass molder, iron molder, brass finisher, pattern maker, steam fitter, and gas fitter.

At age 18, Witte made the unexpected announcement that he was going to further his education by gaining exposure to the manufacturing methods used in New York City. During his 12 months in New York, Witte worked in 20 different shops and saw his first internal combustion engine, one fueled by city gas and rigged to drive machinery. As a child, Witte had ridden the horse that drove a treadmill to power machines in his father's shop. The horse was replaced by a steam engine, which may have contributed to the shop's destruction by fire.

Edward H. Witte

The internal combustion engine that he had seen in New York made a big impression on Ed Witte. When he returned to Kansas City at age 19, the ambitious Witte arranged to buy his father's business. He built and successfully sold a number of steam-driven pumps, but was never confident about the future of such equipment. The increasing availability of gasoline, however, caught Witte's attention. It was, he recognized, a portable fuel that would free internal combustion engines from static hook-ups to city-supplied gas.

According to Edward Witte, his first gasoline engine was a 2 1/2-horsepower, hot-tube ignition machine built in 1887. The following year, Witte sold an engine to the Kansas City Printing Company. Other sales to printers followed as did those to area blacksmiths. With a small sales force, Witte was soon selling 40 engines a month. In October, 1912, Witte, who became famous for his ability to cite the cost and profit of each bolt in every one of his engines, determined that his sales force and dealers were not an economic method of marketing his engines. Instead, he set out upon a quite modern marketing strategy based on direct mail and display ads in newspapers.

It was a highly personal message that Witte now communicated. He put his picture in the ads, wrote the marketing materials using the first person "I" and made his appeal in terms of his own integrity, the proven reliability of his engines, their quality, and their competitive pricing. Once, while on a trip through Colorado, Witte stopped to talk with a farmer carrying a gas can towards an engine. "Why you are old man Witte yourself, now, ain't you?" the farmer exclaimed.

By 1916, Witte was reaching 6 1/2 million people daily and reportedly receiving 5,000 letters a day at the plant. He turned Kansas City's central location and its rail service into a key marketing tool. "We are only 12 to 48 hours away from most of the United States, and but three or four days more away from the farthest corners." Catalogs contained information for shipping

Intake valve | Overflow for fuel pump | Valve chest | Governor | Make-and-break igniter

Fuel intake valve | Fuel cam | Exhaust valve | Exhaust cam | Fuel pump

each engine to different states. In 1913, approximate freight costs to California for a 12-horsepower engine were $49.80 and to New York $21.08.

These Wittes were quality engines, and Ed Witte himself delighted in describing the care and technology that went into each one. His catalogs took prospective customers on a tour through his factory. "In the foundry, skilled workmen form the moulds, using metal non-wearing patterns, and pouring into strong metal flasks in order to get our required uniformity of castings....Our tool room represents more actual money invested in it alone than many so-called modern factories have invested in their whole works."

The catalog stressed the interchangeability of parts, then an important selling point. "A hundred WITTE engines might be taken apart, and all the parts thrown into one pile, and the whole pile mixed up in ever such a bad muddle, yet the engines could all be reassembled and re-erected, using for any engine the first part or parts coming to hand out of the jumble."

The finishing process involved a heavy coat of iron filler, which was allowed to dry and then rubbed down to a smooth surface before being painted with a high-quality enamel and then varnished — "the best that the iron finishers art could make them." In fact, the engine shown here still has 95 percent of its original paint coating. "All I did," said owner Bill Hazzard, "was clean the engine up and re-machine the gasket surfaces on the valve chests because they were warped and leaking. I also took the cylin-

How the Witte Worked

To start the engine, the fuel pump is manually operated to fill the reservoir with gasoline. Then, the cam roller is moved to open the compression release and the cylinder is primed through the priming cup. Then, the battery switch is closed and the flywheels turned until the engine fires. Then, the compression release is closed.

In operation, the fuel valve opens on the intake stroke, letting fuel run into the intake passage. When maximum rpm speed is reached, the hit-or-miss governor moves the fuel cam away from a rocker arm preventing admission of any more fuel.

Special feature note: The connecting rod is adjustable to permit compression to be changed for operation on different fuels.

der head off for the first time in its life and cleaned out about 20 pounds of rust from the water jacket." This experience suggests that Witte's policy of having overly large water jackets to compensate for the buildup of "mud" was successful.

Oddly enough, considering that Witte developed his engine during a period when patents and patent suits were very much the order of the day, he never sought patent protection himself. An article in *The Gas Engine* magazine even noted that "everyone is entitled to build the engine." As a practical matter, of course, the intellectual capital and manufacturing resources supporting Witte's enterprise were as vital to his success as any particular detail of the engine itself.

The business quite literally boomed. Exhaust pipes extending through the walls of the factory test department emitted the sharp cracks of the smaller engines, and the measured staccato reverberations of the bigger ones. A Japanese businessman arranged to sell the Witte engine in Japan, and other export markets opened up, too. Early in World War I, a Russian count appeared in Kansas City to purchase engines for use in the trenches. These Wittes were equipped with special mufflers and were to be operated while cocooned in heavy burlap in an effort to keep their positions secret from German artillery. By 1923, there were factory branches in San Francisco and in Pittsburgh.

Witte began research on diesel engines in the early '30s and produced his first production diesel in 1934. Most were used to power generators and thousands were used during the war on Landing Ship Tank (LST) craft and on barges. Some 350 employees were employed at Witte during World War II and they worked in one of the most modern glass and concrete factories in the city. The business was running smoothly when, at age 76, Witte sold it to the Oil Well Supply Company, a Dallas subsidiary of U.S. Steel.

As for Edward Witte himself, he is remembered not only as a successful engine man and progressive employer who issued stock to the workers, but as a generous philanthropist. His one interest outside the plant was an 817 acre farm that he and his wife Ida used as a both a hobby and a retreat. In 1923, Witte offered the farm to the Brotherhood of American Yeoman as the site for a proposed children's home. "My wife and I have talked it over," Witte told a newspaper reporter that January. "We have no children. That farm was made for children. We want to see children play in those groves. We want to see children fish in those lakes. It ought to be."

Muffler

Pushrod for exhaust valve

Governor spring

Needle valve

Mixer

Choke plate

Fuel line

GRAY MOTOR CO DETROIT

In April, 1904, in recognition of the increasing role that gasoline engines were playing on the American farm, the Iowa State College of Agriculture and Mechanical Arts established a new department called "Farm Mechanics." A fire-proof building was erected to house several gasoline engines loaned by various manufacturers, and there, students began to learn the mysteries of internal combustion.

By the time the College began offering formal instruction in the subject, gasoline engines had already made steady inroads on the steam engine and the windmill among American farmers. Articles in *The Gas Engine* regularly compared the efficiency and cost of these traditional power sources with those of a gasoline engine, always to the latter's advantage. But it was an economic advantage quickly grasped by the farmers themselves. Gasoline engines were employed to run wood saws, fodder cutters, corn shellers, churns, cream separators, sheep shearing machines, grinders, and, of course, for pumping water.

All this potential usefulness created an enormous demand, enough to support literally hundreds upon hundreds of engine manufacturers whose primary market was the American farmer. Up in Detroit, Michigan, at the Gray Motor Company, Ora J. Mulford recognized that the potential demand for "farm engines" exceeded by far that of his first love, marine motors. Gray introduced a stationary version of its classic, two-cycle marine engine in 1909. One version was developed for pumping applications, another for electrical work, and another to run machines of various sorts. It was reported that a four-horsepower model used on a rice binder replaced five mules in harvesting 120 acres.

In 1911, Gray introduced a new model developed exclusively for stationary applications. The engine was quite probably a concerted effort to capitalize on the inherent size of the market for such engines compared to that for marine engines. And it was a matter of survival, too. In 1910, Gray, which had been acquired only a year earlier by the automobile maker, United States Motor Company, went bankrupt. Mulford bought back the engine side of the business and immediately sought ways to overcome the debt he acquired in doing so. The engine shown here was a key part of the plan.

Gray called its new portable farm engine the "Thoroughbred" and Mulford, who made his serious money writing ads for Henry Ford, Packard, and others, turned his pen to his latest product. "No better workmanship in $5,000 automobiles," said the ad brochures. The Thoroughbred was available in 2 1/2- and four-horsepower models (Model G) and more powerful versions all the way up to the 25 horsepower Model O.

The company noted, however, that "the 4 H. P. engine is the best and most serviceable all around power size the farmer can buy today." Said the Gray catalog: "A 4 H. P. will do every job on the farm except running the biggest threshers and silo blowers…. Hundreds of Gray 4 H. P.'s are used for threshing in the southern states and parts of Canada where smaller threshing machines are used. The Thoroughbred will pump water, separate milk….It is light enough to be portable and will last a life time. A strong boy can pull it around on our sturdy, wide tired hand truck."

A lot of people who read that copy bought Gray motors, among them the engine shown here. The Thoroughbred's gasoline tank was in the base. The hopper that was part of the cylinder casting (to prevent leaks) contained the cooling water. The casting was subjected to an hydraulic pressure test to insure against possible leakage. Said the company, "Gray hoppers are all large. They are deep and the full length of the cylinder. They have big radiating surfaces. The opening has a non-splashing flange cast in it. They don't boil over unless filled to the brim, which is not necessary." The engine was mounted on "well-seasoned wood skids" which also carried the battery box.

The Model G shown here is remarkably original in all respects, including its drip feed oil lubricators. (There are no grease cups.) It was used to drive a small feed grinder on a New England farm and, according to its owner, "appears never to have been left outside."

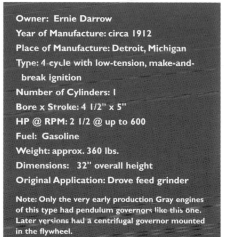

Owner: Ernie Darrow
Year of Manufacture: circa 1912
Place of Manufacture: Detroit, Michigan
Type: 4-cycle with low-tension, make-and-break ignition
Number of Cylinders: 1
Bore x Stroke: 4 1/2" x 5"
HP @ RPM: 2 1/2 @ up to 600
Fuel: Gasoline
Weight: approx. 360 lbs.
Dimensions: 32" overall height
Original Application: Drove feed grinder

Note: Only the very early production Gray engines of this type had pendulum governors like this one. Later versions had a centrifugal governor mounted in the flywheel.

PALMER BROTHERS

Owner: Ernie Darrow
Manufacturer: Palmer Brothers
Year of Manufacture: Circa 1919
Place of Manufacture: Cos Cob, Connecticut
Type: 2-cycle
Fuel: Gasoline
Ignition: Spark plug and buzz coil
Number of Cylinders: 1
Bore x Stroke: 7" x 10"
HP @ RPM: 2 @ 500
Weight: 135 lbs.
Dimensions: 13" flywheel; 13" Height
Original Application: Marine

Frank and Ray Palmer grew up in Greenwich, Connecticut, the sons of a father who owned one of the state's largest cider mills. The brothers attended public school in Greenwich, and spent as much spare time as possible rowing and sailing in Cos Cob Harbor and Long Island Sound. In 1888, when Frank Palmer was 31 years old and Ray 28, the two young men opened a shop in North Mianus where they made telephones and electrical equipment.

According to family lore, Ray Palmer saw his first marine internal combustion engine in 1890. It would be intriguing to know what this engine was, although the lack of possibilities suggest it was most likely a Sintz. Whatever it was, Palmer decided he could do better. During the next several years, the Palmers steadily developed a little two-port, two-cycle engine fed by a primitive vaporizer through a one-inch pipe. A gate-type air valve required frequent adjustment, and those who witnessed the early days of Palmer development recalled seeing the brothers rocking their boat from side to side to assist the vaporizer in delivering its 80 octane fumes to the engine. Most important for the future, however, was the engine's make-and-break igniter. As refined by Ray Palmer, this igniter was central to what became a quite dramatic success. Its positive action provided reliable ignition, one of the key stumbling blocks at the time.

In 1894, the Palmers began producing and selling a little 1 1/2-horsepower motor and shortly thereafter, a three-horsepower model. According to a 1906 article in The Motor Boat, the engines, built at a rate of three or four a week for the first couple of years, had an impact far beyond their modest physical size. For one thing, the Palmers made the engine available as castings to those who wanted to build their own motor, a task that was widely encouraged by the press of the day as the best way for a boater to learn internal combustion. Thus, whatever secrets lay within the engine's castings were soon known to virtually anyone who cared. But it was the make-and-break igniter, according to The Motor Boat "that has been more extensively copied by other builders of gas engines than any other feature of the marine motor."

Being widely imitated did nothing to curtail the success of Palmer Brothers. Their engines worked reliably and easily and word spread fast, first among local oyster fishermen and then pleasure operators. The brothers found themselves having to continually expand their factory until finally, in 1901, they bought a four-acre site in Cos Cob on the Mianus River and built the plant that would be famous for decades to come. Five or six years later, output was some 40 engines per week, with Ray Palmer overseeing the technical side and Frank the company management.

By 1910, 500 people were employed at Palmer. Not all were engaged in building engines. The brothers had learned that recreational boaters became more likely buyers if they could simply purchase the complete boat, and the Palmers offered a full line of stock launches. By 1907, these ranged in size from a $188, 1 1/2-horsepower 17-footer to a $600, seven-horsepower, 30-footer. (For comparison's sake, a 1907 Ford Model S Runabout cost $750.) Said the catalog: "With every boat we send oil can, can of cylinder oil, bearing grease and batteries." The brothers also produced dredge hoisters for use aboard oyster boats, a wood-sawing machine, whistles, "magneto sparkers," a reverse gear, and a twin-flywheel, stationary engine.

The little Palmer shown here is a Model Q introduced in 1906. Although fishermen had no need for higher speed than that offered by the traditional two-port Palmer with its check valve that admitted mixture to the base, the Q was a three-port. The Palmers were among those who paid a license fee to British engineer Joseph Day whose patent on the three-port two-cycle engine was still in effect. The three-port design, which required no check valve, allowed the "motor to run at much higher speed."

It's worth noting that the Model Q pictured in the Palmer catalog for 1907 was clearly not a three-port engine even though the copy implied that it was. According to Palmer authority Dick Day, the "Q started out as a two-port engine apparently some time prior to 1906. They made it into a three-port engine in 1906 but the engine actually shown in the 1907 catalog is a two-port not a three-port."

The gear-driven timer was introduced in 1907. The engine pictured is original in all respects including its true, "Palmer blue-gray" paint color.

The Engine Named for a Road

SPEEDWAY

Owner: Tim James
Manufacturer: Consolidated Shipbuilding
Company
Year of Manufacture: 1920
Place of Manufacture: Morris Heights, New York
Type: 4-cycle
Fuel: Gasoline
Ignition: Triple plugs (Bosch two-spark magneto
and Delco distributor)
Number of Cylinders: 6
Bore x Stroke: 5 3/4" x 7"
HP @ RPM: 75 – 130 @ 600 – 1,000
Weight: 2,400 lbs.
Dimensions: 88.5" long x 28" wide x 44" high
Original Application: Power for 60-foot launch

As marine engine development progressed in the last few years leading up to America's entry into World War I, the basic appearance of the engines underwent a dramatic evolution. The engine shown here, introduced to the public in April, 1916, was a good example of the change. Its sleek appearance said it all. "The engine is of the enclosed type," noted *Motor Boating*," giving a noiseless, compact and smooth running unit. The cylinders are cast in pairs, of the L-head type with integral heads and jackets.... The engine is started by an electric starting system."

The engine was the Speedway Model M and it represented a future that was as inevitable as the tides. Open crankcases, make-and-break ignition, exposed cams or gears, even the bulky, classic T-head configuration were all gradually fading into memory. Customers fitting out pleasure cruisers and runabouts wanted convenience, quiet operation, reliability, and neat engine compartments. The big new Speedway gave it to them.

Its maker classed this 600 – 1000-rpm version as "medium duty" during an era when the terms high duty or high speed, medium duty, and heavy duty were routinely advertised and widely debated. The Speedway high duty Model M was rated at 1,000 – 1,200 rpm, had an aluminum base, and was intended for applications like speed boats and runabouts where speed was paramount. The medium duty rating shown here had an iron base and 600 – 1,000 rpm rating. The heavy-duty model was rated at 300 – 500 rpm and was suitable for commercial service, houseboats, and heavier cruising yachts. Later, in 1923, the MR was introduced. It had removable cylinder heads housing single overhead valves resulting in an increase in maximum horsepower from 130 to 185 horsepower.

"The MR engine has not been produced to supplant the model M," reported the company, "but to amplify the complete line of Speedway engines, which now comprises eleven different models ranging in power from 22 to 300 hp."

This quite modern marine engine was built by a company whose history dated back to the days of steam power and the naptha-powered launches developed by a German-born genius named F. W. Ofeldt. It was Ofeldt who attracted the backing of Jabez

along the river dominated by fast-moving carriages and horsemen.

Speedway engines were well known to wealthy yachtsmen. One of them was Francis Frink, proprietor of the Washington Iron Works on Seattle's Lake Union. In 1919, the *Pacific Motor Boat* published an article about the new 55-foot boat then being built for Frink to a design by naval architect L. E. Geary. The boat was powered by a Speedway Model M, the very same type shown here. Today, Frink's old yacht is owned by Tim James who, when the vessel's restoration is complete, will install this Model M in the engine room. Such a move is highly unusual; almost all restored boats are repowered with modern engines, usually diesels, that forever alter their original character.

This particular Speedway had originally powered a 60-foot cruiser owned by a wealthy New York area couple. When found by marine engine specialist Danny Acierno, the engine was in need of total restoration but it was 90 percent complete. Recognizing the ambitious and important nature of Tim James's project, and his desire to repower the ex-Frink yacht with the original-specification engine, Acierno sold Tim the old Speedway. When complete, Tim's boat will be one-of-a-kind, a living monument to one of the country's earliest and most famous marine engine and boat builders, and to a long-past age of American yachting.

Bostwick, the proprietor of a company on 131st Street in New York City called The Gas Engine and Power Company. Bostwick, who was connected to the Standard Oil Company, began the company to produce stationary engines, but its location on the Harlem River in what was then known as Morris Heights, made it well-suited to marine endeavors. In the decade between 1885 and 1895, it was estimated that the company built and sold some 3,000 naptha engines and launches.

Ofeldt had a falling out with the management and went on to other engine endeavors, but in 1895, according to the memory of naval architect L. Francis Herreshoff, the steam yacht designer and builder from Nyack, New York, Charles L. Seabury, joined the firm. Thus resulted the cumbersome name — The Gas Engine & Power Company, and Charles L. Seabury & Company, Consolidated. In 1919, the name was changed to be the well-known label, Consolidated Shipbuilding Company. Names aside, this was a prosperous enterprise. By the time the Model M was introduced, the Consolidated factory occupied a plant with 1,800 feet of river frontage. It was a big business with enough employees to justify a monthly company newspaper, the *Speedway News*. The engines (and a car, too, built in 1904–1905) took their name from the road

Originally built in 1919 for Francis Frink, a proprietor of Seattle's Washington Iron Works, this 55-foot power cruiser was equipped with a six-cylinder Speedway built by Consolidated in Morris Heights, New York. The boat could carry 700 gallons of fuel. It was originally painted green below the waterline, and black above, with a white boot top and gold leaf cove stripe. (Courtesy of Tim James)

The Fisherman's Friend

HICKS

The Hicks make-and-break igniters are easily replaced by a distributor and sparkplug ignition system (Courtesy of Christopher Seats)

Owner: Christopher Werner Seitz and Albert E. Lampi
Name of Manufacturer: Yuba Manufacturing Company
Year of Manufacture: Circa 1925 - 1930
Place of Manufacture: Benecia, California
Type: 4-cycle
Fuel: Gasoline
Ignition: Sumter magneto and Fahnestock igniters or six-volt battery, distributor and Champion A-25 spark plugs
Number of Cylinders: 4
Bore x Stroke: 6.05" x 6.60"
HP @ RPM: 18 @ 350 – 27 @ 500
Weight: 2,700 lbs.
Dimensions: 9' long x 6' high x 2' wide
Original Application: Power for 36-foot Monterey-style fishing vessel

The exposed nature of the coast around San Francisco with its strong currents and winds, and the great expanse of the Pacific itself, all combined to influence the development of the classic California marine engine. In contrast to the two-cycle engines so common in New England and the Canadian Maritimes, the engines built on the West Coast were heavy-duty four-cycle types. They were capable of pushing a heavily built boat day-in and day-out while needing rather little attention. Such engines were built by Union, Atlas, Imperial, Samson, Standard, and, beginning in 1892, by J. L. Hicks Machine Tools and Gas Engines.

The classic Hicks was an eight-horsepower single-cylinder engine with a make-and-break ignition system impervious to moisture. Installed in the Monterey Clipper, this was the staple power for the Italian-American fisherman on San Francisco's waterfront. By the time the Hicks family sold the company to the Yuba Manufacturing Company in 1927, advertising claimed that "Over 80% of the fishing boats using six-

to thirty-five horsepower engines in California waters are equipped with Hicks engines."

The engine pictured here spent all its working life in a fishing boat, too, but that it did was an accident of history. In this case, the accident involved the U.S. Navy. Almost since the internal combustion engine became viable, the Navy had been a customer of diverse manufacturers. The Otto Engine Company in Philadelphia supplied gasoline engines for the *U.S.S. Holland* and

The fishing vessel, Chaser, a scaled-up Monterey style boat, was first powered by a two-cylinder Hicks and later the three-cylinder pictured here.

Compression release · Upper water manifold · Exhaust manifold · Hand oil prime · Shift lever

Check valves

Water manifold · Pressure oil lines · Raw water piston pump · Sea cock

other submarines, and a variety of other companies contracted with the Navy to build engines that went into all manner of naval small craft. The Navy even manufactured engines on its own at the Norfolk Navy Yard, some under license and others of its own design.

This particular engine was purchased by the Navy, most probably in the late '20s or early '30s, for installation at the Mare Island Naval Shipyard. It differs from production Hicks models of the time in that is

equipped with three carburetors instead of one. Also, its make-and-break igniters can be replaced by a six-volt Autolite conversion with a drop-in distributor. But the Navy never used this Hicks. Late in 1933, the Navy finally acted on a concern that had been expressed since its very first purchase of a gasoline engine — safety. It announced a plan to "dieselize" its entire fleet of small craft. This would prove to be a big project, since at least 1,800 boats of various types and powers were involved. Now, gasoline engines in existing boats began to be replaced by Navy-built Buda diesels.

At Mare Island in 1939, the Hicks was sold as surplus to fishermen Herb and Frank Fraham. They promptly removed the two-cylinder, 1918-vintage Hicks from their boat *Chaser* and replaced it with this one. *Chaser* was a scaled-up Monterey Clipper built by Werner Swain and well-adapted to the rugged conditions of Humboldt Bay. For the next three decades, the Hicks faithfully powered the 36-foot *Chaser* until it was replaced when the boat was restored and repowered in 1976.

Manzel oiler

Splitdorf magneto

Igniter pushrod

Igniter

Unlike many old marine engines, the Hicks was kept largely intact by Albert Lampi, *Chaser's* new owner. Even its original gasoline tank and the bronze lags supplied to fasten the engine to its timber bed were saved. Although it had been running on its distributor-style ignition system, most parts for the mechanical igniters had also been saved. By 1985, the engine was residing in Mr. Lampi's shed where it was purchased by a Hicks enthusiast and research vessel captain named Chris Seitz. Over the next 10 years, Seitz began a loving restoration of each and every piece of the engine.

It was a project any engine collector would understand. The bedplate was sand-blasted and primed and the bearings were scraped. The crankshaft was repolished and the cylinders were machined. The oil pump was disassembled and rebuilt as were each of the three carburetors. Seitz, who had also been a gunsmith, reblued all the minor steel parts and primed and painted the others. Any missing parts were refabricated to original specifications until finally, the engine assumed the form in which it is seen here. Today, the old Hicks stands as an evocative reminder of a time when fishermen went to sea with simple, reliable, and long-lived gasoline engines that had so revolutionized their age-old craft.

Starting the Hicks

After filling the oil tank, the hand crank is used to feed oil to the cylinders and bearings. An oil can is used to lube the raw water pump, cam shaft, and valve train. Next, the sea valve on the engine's port side aft is opened to admit cooling water. With the engine now ready to run, each priming cup atop the cylinders is filled with gasoline. Then the choke levers on the carburetors are closed and each is flooded. The compression release is partially opened using the front handle on the rocker shaft and the throttle is opened part way. The timing is retarded by moving the lever forward. The engine is now ready to go. A 3/4" pipe starting handle is inserted into the flywheel cutout and the engine is slowly turned counter-clockwise until any igniter lever contacts its pawl. Then, says owner Seitz, "You jump down on the pipe starter handle and pray." With the engine running, the compression release is closed and the spark advanced.

The Pioneer Diesel from Oakland

ATLAS-IMPERIAL

Fuel pressure gauge

Sight feed pressure lubricator

Exhaust pushrod

Injector pushrod

Air Valve pushrod

Intake pushrod

Fuel pressure adjuster lever

Oil pump   Oil pressure gauge   Governor   Throttle

How the Atlas-Imperial Worked

Fuel was injected by spray valves (injectors) at a pressure of 1,000 to 3,500 psi. The pressure was developed by plunger pumps operated by cranks mounted on the camshaft. The injectors were supplied by a fuel line — the "common rail" of the system — which carried fuel pumped from the tank through a strainer to hold back impurities. Said Atlas-Imperial: " A branch pipe connects each spray nozzle to the high pressure oil system. An additional branch leads to a pressure regulator and relief valve, which regulates the pressure, and by-passes all oil not required to maintain constant pressure....The spray valve is mechanically opened by a cam and properly TIMED with the cycles of operation to gradually inject the fuel at the proper time for ignition." The only air required for operation was that used for starting.

Owner: Bob Hardin
Manufacturer: Atlas-Imperial Diesel Engine Company
Year of Manufacture: Circa 1918 - 1926
Place of Manufacture: Oakland, California
Type: Mechanical injection, 4-cycle diesel
Fuel: Diesel
Number of Cylinders: 3
HP @ RPM: 65 @ 250 - 350
Weight: 11,000 lbs.
Dimensions: 38" flywheel
Original Application: Marine

Three pioneering California engine builders selected for their engines names that would convey images of great strength: Hercules, Samson, and Atlas. The latter had just started building its big, rugged, gasoline engines in San Francisco when the earthquake struck in 1906 and wiped out the whole business. Atlas then received an infusion of capital and moved from its original site across the bay to Oakland.

Shortly after the earthquake, the Imperial Gas Engine Company was also begun. Like Atlas, a primary focus was marine engines. These developed into quite interesting machines with overhead valves and an overhead camshaft and, for the next decade, the company's products and aspirations rather closely paralleled those of Atlas. Then, beginning about 1911 or 1912, with gasoline prices on the rise and the cost of operating a big gasoline engine moving up fast, both engine makers realized they had better do something. In 1916, Atlas and Imperial merged to form Atlas-Imperial, a name that would soon gain fame all along the Pacific Coast.

In 1914, when Atlas began development work of its first diesel, such engines required a compressor, air tanks, and piping as part of the fuel injection system. The many air system components required continual maintenance and the piping and joints were always subject to leaks. The compressors sapped engine power, too. The glory that was Atlas-Imperial grew out of a new fuel system that eliminated all the problems of the air-injected diesel and made possible what, in that epoch, could reasonably be called by Atlas-Imperial "small or medium-sized full Diesel type engines." The first three diesels that Atlas-Imperial built, beginning in 1916, were air-injection engines. But then in 1919 the company, most probably with an eye on development in England at Vickers, announced its first engine that did away with the troublesome air

system. This was the soon to be famous "common rail" or "mechanical injection" diesel engine.

Thus began the great "Iron Age" of the marine diesel. These gentle giants produced great power at a leisurely 250 – 350 rpm and they made good on Atlas-Imperial's claim of operating costs that were only 10 percent that of a comparable gasoline engine. Atlas-Imperial now entered a golden era that saw nearly every seiner and cannery tender from California to Alaska equipped with one of its engines. In 1928, actor John Barrymore fitted his big schooner yacht with a 120 horsepower Atlas-Imperial. Others followed suit. There were some important land-based applications for Atlas as well. Industrialist Henry J. Kaiser replaced a gasoline engine in a Caterpillar tractor with an Atlas in 1927. All this prompted Atlas to develop enclosed versions of the engine whose workings would be protected from dust and dirt.

During the two decades leading up to World War II, Atlas-Imperial ranked as one of the country's most important engine makers. But, with the advent of GM's high-speed, lightweight, less expensive diesels shortly before World War II, the classic Atlas-Imperial passed into history. Still, of the thousands that had once faithfully powered legions of working craft, some engines did survive. The engine shown here is in every way complete and original. It is an evocative reminder of the simple marine diesel that was much admired as a faithful shipmate by generations of engine men.

The Pride of Bridgeport

WOLVERINE

Owner: Capt. Lawrence Mahan

Year of Manufacture: 1928

Place of Manufacture: Bridgeport, Connecticut

Type: 4-cycle diesel

Number of Cylinders: 4

Bore x Stroke: 8 5/8" x 12"

HP @ RPM: 100 @ 350

Weight: 14,700 lbs.

Dimensions: 11' long x 5' tall

Original Application: Fishing vessel

Charles L. Snyder as he appeared in about 1917.
(Courtesy of Capt. Larry Mahan)

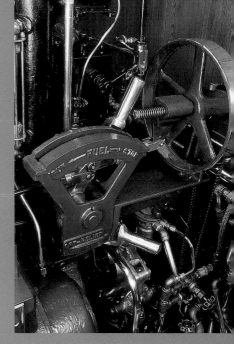

"There was a time," engineer Claude Sintz told an interviewer in 1952, "when the sun never set on the Wolverine motor." Sintz was in a good position to know. Although he was then 76 and in his final year, he still clearly remembered the day in 1894 when, as a 19-year old, he and his father Clark founded Wolverine. The company was located in Grand Rapids, Michigan, where it replaced as a Sintz family business the recently sold Sintz Gas Engine Company. Wolverine's initial product was a two-cycle engine, the patent for which was registered in Claude's name. Within a half-dozen years, these engines had succeeded on a wide scale. From Iceland to Tasmania, Wolverines were in widespread use.

Among the earliest and most satisfied Wolverine customers was a wealthy entrepreneur who, with his brothers, was busily creating the basis of a substantial fortune as a pioneer in the banana growing and exporting industry in Panama. This man was Charles Snyder. It was Snyder who recognized the labor-saving potential of an internal combustion marine engine as a replacement for the row boats used to transport bananas along the rivers linking the plantations and shipping points. Initially, two of the Snyders' banana-hauling launches were fitted with a Wolverine two-cycle engine. Their success generated orders for six more. In 1895, Snyder visited the Sintzs at Grand Rapids. There he remained for several months, collaborating with Clark and Claude on a gasoline-powered, narrow gauge locomotive that would operate on a network of newly laid track on the largest of the Snyder plantations.

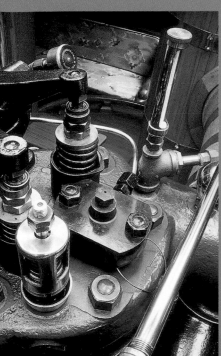

The success of the Wolverine engine and Charles Snyder's good relationship with the inventive Sintzs would have profound implications for both. In 1889, Snyder and his brothers concluded a deal to sell their business to the United Fruit Company. It was a big sale and Charles used a portion of his wealth to purchase Wolverine in 1900. In 1907, to better access export markets, Snyder moved the company to Bridgeport, Connecticut, commencing a business that would remain a vital landmark in the city for a half century. The end came for Wolverine, as it did for all the pioneering marine engine companies that had survived World War II, in the mid-'50s. Service and parts continued to be offered until 1972 under a subsequent owner, the Coulter McKenzie Machine Company. Finally, the remaining assets of the old company, comprising some 16 tons of parts, were purchased in 1982 by a long-time Wolverine enthusiast in Massachusetts named Larry Mahan.

At that time Mahan was deeply involved in the slow but steady realization of a remarkable lifelong dream. The result, some 18 years later, was the completion of a thoroughly unique sailing vessel whose auxiliary power is supplied by the Wolverine diesel engine pictured here. "We found the engine in a Connecticut salvage yard," Mahan says of the Wolverine. "The crankcase was full of leaves and dirt and the cylinders were scattered around in the mud."

Thus began a decade-long restoration project. The result is a perfectly functioning example of a machine from the great "Iron Age" of diesel technology. Massive, slow-turning, reliable, this old Wolverine stands as the solution to the many problems that had confronted diesel engine designers who sought to develop a machine that would be freed from the complex and none too functional air injection systems needed on previous engines. During the mid-teens, companies like Atlas-Imperial on the West Coast, and Wolverine in New England were hard at work on a solution to the problem. At Wolverine, diesel research was begun about 1915 and the Wolverine fuel system is based on mechanical injectors developed by company engineer Ralph Booth. Each cylinder is equipped with an individually adjustable injector fed by a central pump. "You can adjust fuel by cylinder with a pyrometer," says Mahan, "making it possible to ideally balance each one."

The factory of the Wolverine Motor Works was built at 35 Union Ave. in Bridgeport, Connecticut, in 1907. (Courtesy of Capt. Larry Mahan)

Snyder family connection with the old company passed in 1954 with the death of Charles Snyder's son Louis, Sr. in 1954.

Larry Mahan's restoration of this Wolverine is unusual not merely for its quality but for the fact that the engine is in daily use fulfilling the function for which it was designed some 75 years ago. Visitors may encounter the Wolverine aboard the schooner *Larinda* — a vessel as thoroughly remarkable as her owner — during her seasonal cruises and tall ship appearances all along the East Coast.

Mahan's Wolverine employs an exhaust system that is installed within the main mast, which is conveniently located just ahead of the engine. The exhaust pipe extends 15 feet up the mast and the result is wonderfully quiet operation. A big, brightly polished brass remote oil tank stands at the starboard rear of the Wolverine, and the engine is cooled by a freshwater system that protects the cylinders from the potentially damaging corrosion of salt water.

Reflecting on the cessation of production at Wolverine in the summer of 1955, the company's then president Milton Friedberg stated what had become obvious to everyone since the introduction by General Motors of its high-speed diesel engines. "There is no demand for heavy duty diesel engines such as the company manufactures," he told the *Bridgeport Post*. "The cutback in the workforce will be gradual." The last

How the Wolverine Worked

Starting commences after oiling of key wear points such as the ends of the exposed pushrods. The Wolverine operates as a conventional, four-cycle compression-ignition diesel. However, when the engine is cold, starting is aided by heating each cylinder. This is accomplished by placing a piece of waste cloth inside a removable, thread-in plug fitted to each cylinder head. The cloth is lit and the plug screwed back into the head.

To start the Wolverine, the throttle, controlled by a wheel on the engine's port side, is opened a third of the way. Next, the compression releases atop each cylinder are simultaneously opened by another lever. Finally, a lever is operated that admits compressed air to all cylinders in sequence. The compression releases are shut after the Wolverine starts, usually on the third revolution. It turns a 42" adjustable propeller.

Four-cylinder Wolverine diesel, 1932. The standard paint color was "Egyptian gray" but any color could be ordered. Some Wolverines were built with many parts made of stainless steel. (Courtesy of Capt. Larry Mahan)